# Concerning Himself

J T Mawson

**Scripture Truth Publications**

## CONCERNING HIMSELF

Revised and reprinted from a series entitled "Things Most Surely Believed" in "Scripture Truth" magazine, Volumes 26-27, 1934-35, and an additional article from Volume 28, 1936.

First published 1936 by Marshall, Morgan & Scott, London & Edinburgh and The Central Bible Truth Depôt, 5 Rose Street, Paternoster Square, London, E.C.4

Re-typeset with amended/additional references and transferred to Digital Printing 2014

ISBN: 978-0-901860-92-7 (paperback)

Copyright © 2014 Scripture Truth Publications

A publication of Scripture Truth

All rights reserved. No part of this publication may be reproduced, stored in a retrieval system, or transmitted, in any form or by any means, electronic, mechanical, photocopying, recording or otherwise without prior permission of Scripture Truth Publications.

Scripture quotations, unless otherwise indicated, are taken from The Authorized (King James) Version. Rights in the Authorized Version are vested in the Crown. Reproduced by permission of the Crown's patentee, Cambridge University Press.

Scripture quotations marked "RV" are taken from "The Holy Bible, Revised Version", Oxford: University Press, 1885

Scripture quotations marked "N.Tr." are taken from "The Holy Scriptures, a New Translation from the Original Languages" by J. N. Darby (G Morrish, 1890)

Cover photograph ©iStockphoto.com/Ynot2 (Gilad Levy)

Published by Scripture Truth Publications
31-33 Glover Street, Crewe, Cheshire, CW1 3LD

*Scripture Truth is an imprint of Central Bible Hammond Trust, a charitable trust*

Typesetting by John Rice
Printed by Lightning Source

## Preface to the 2014 Edition

Christianity is all about Christ, and unless He is the all-absorbing Subject of each Christian's life then, as John Owen wrote in *Christologia* as long ago as 1679, "whatever outward ornaments may be put upon its exercise, it is but a useless, lifeless carcass".

But where do we learn of Christ? On the opening page of the first issue of *Scripture Truth* in January 1909 its joint editors, J. T. Mawson and H. D. R. Jameson, were certain as they wrote, "The Scriptures will always be prized by the children of God, not only because they come from God, but because they speak of Christ, and indeed it is only as this is seen, and Christ is loved, that they are understood. We shall endeavour, as time and space permit, to draw out from the Scriptures the things concerning Christ, believing that the surest way of preservation from the seductive movements, doctrines, and spirits that abound, is occupation with that which is good; for 'who is he that shall harm you, if ye be followers of that which is good' (1 Peter 3:13). All good is centred in, and flows from Christ; and it is as He is paramount in the lives of His people, that they are happy themselves and useful to others. Then Christianity becomes a reality—no longer visionary, but practical; no longer mere doctrine for the mind (important as that is), but power in the life."

# CONCERNING HIMSELF

Over more than 30 years, as he edited and contributed to *Scripture Truth*, J. T. Mawson was as good as his word, 'drawing out from the Scriptures the things concerning Christ'. The present volume contains thirteen inspirational articles on exactly this theme.

To assist the twenty-first century reader, minor changes in presentation have been made. The use of quotation (speech) marks has been updated. Scripture references have been checked and the full title of the book is provided, to facilitate ease of lookup. Some references have been added to scriptures quoted, because not all today are as familiar with the Bible as those of J. T. Mawson's generation. Details of other publications referred to in the text are given at the end of the book. Otherwise the text has not been changed.

The publishers commend this book to you. May it help your appreciation of the Lord Jesus Christ to grow more each day.

*John Rice*

## Author's Preface

### THE WORD OF GOD

With the true Church of God on earth, I believe in God and *the Word of His Grace*, and I am persuaded that if "God so loved the world that He gave His only-begotten Son, that whosoever believeth in Him should not perish, but have everlasting life", He would see to it that we should be in no uncertainty about it, else how could any man have said, "Thanks be unto God for His unspeakable gift"?

If the only-begotten Son of God, divinely perfect and blessed, came into the world and lived and died and rose again from the dead for the blessing of men, God must of necessity give men a record of this, also divinely perfect and blessed, that those for whom He came might have a divine and perfect assurance of it. Admit the former and the latter follows in logical sequence.

To suppose that God would send His only-begotten Son into the world that we might live through Him, and having done that allow an imperfect, contradictory human record to be the only record of His life and death and resurrection would be to suppose Him guilty of colossal folly. The record must be as perfect in its sphere as the One whose life and mission it records was perfect in His, or else we have no sure knowledge, no certainty about these things upon which our souls' eternal welfare depends.

The Holy Scriptures are God-breathed; the men who wrote them were moved by the Holy Ghost; they had the things they wrote, not from hearsay, nor from their own imperfect observation, though they did declare what they had seen and heard (1 John 1), but they did this as guided and instructed by the Holy Ghost, for, said their Lord, "The Comforter, which is the Holy Ghost, whom the Father will send in My Name, He shall teach you all things, and bring all things to your remembrance whatsoever I have said unto you" (John 14:26).

The Holy Scriptures are the Word of God to us; to them we turn for light and instruction as to Christ and His work. Old and New Testament bear their united testimony to Him, and the revelation that they give is wholly satisfying.

In this small volume I have endeavoured to open up the Scriptures that speak of Him. He did this Himself on the day of His resurrection. When walking with two of His disciples who did not recognise Him, He said to them, "O fools, and slow of heart to believe *all* that the prophets have spoken: ought not Christ to have suffered these things, and to enter into His glory? And beginning at Moses and *all* the prophets He expounded unto them in *all* the Scriptures the things CONCERNING HIMSELF" (Luke 24:25-27).

The Word of God is the only authority upon which I base the assurance with which I have written of these things, and by the Word of God alone what I have written must be tested and judged.

*J. T. Mawson*

## Contents

Preface to the 2014 Edition ......................................... 3

Author's Preface ......................................................... 5

1. The Miraculous Birth:
   The Fact and the Reason for It ........................... 9

2. The Deity of the Lord Jesus:
   The Necessity for It ............................................. 23

3. The Deity of the Lord Jesus:
   In the Opening of the New Testament ............. 35

4. The Sinlessness of the Lord Jesus:
   Why it Must Be .................................................. 47

5. The Temptations of the Lord Jesus:
   What Their Character Was ................................ 57

6. The Miracles of the Lord Jesus:
   What They Prove ................................................ 73

7. The Deity of the Lord Jesus:
   In the Gospel of John ......................................... 85

8. The Death of the Lord Jesus:
   Atonement by Blood .......................................... 97

9. The Resurrection of the Lord Jesus:
   God's Seal upon His Work ............................... 109

10. The Exaltation of the Lord Jesus:
    The Answer to His Humiliation ...................... 121

11. Our Great High Priest:
    His Qualification for the Office ...................... 131

12. The Deity of the Lord Jesus:
    In the Later Epistles ......................................... 143

13. The Son of Man:
    The Judge of Quick and Dead ......................... 155

References ............................................................ 167

# The Miraculous Birth
## THE FACT AND THE REASON FOR IT

## CONCERNING HIMSELF

Men who have pledged themselves to preach and testify to "the Faith once delivered to the saints" have become bold and more bold in rejecting the truth as to our Lord's entrance into the world. To quote from one of them: "I cannot help including the birth stories among the things that do not matter. There are some things that matter a great deal. There are some life and death matters, if it comes to that, but this is not one of them. It does not matter."

It is my purpose to show that it does matter, that it is one of the foundation stones of our faith, and that, apart from it, the whole edifice of the truth must collapse and fall.

# Chapter 1
# The Miraculous Birth

### The Fact and the Reason for It

Many are the names and titles that describe the person and glories of our Lord Jesus Christ in the New Testament. He is the Word who was with God in the beginning, and who was God; the Creator of all things, the Giver of universal life and the Light of men; He is the only-begotten Son which is in the bosom of the Father, His Beloved, in whom is all His delight; He is the Resurrection and the Life; He is the brightness of God's glory and the express image of His Person, who upholds all things by the word of His power; He is the wisdom of God, the power of God and the Lord of glory, the Christ, who is over all, God blessed for ever, having an everlasting throne and ruling with a righteous sceptre; He is the Same yesterday, to-day, and for ever; He is the Root and the Offspring of David, the Alpha and the Omega, the First and the Last, the Beginning and the End; He is the Lamb of God which taketh away the sin of the world, the Bread of God and of life, the Door of Salvation, the Son of Man with power on earth to forgive sins; He is the only Saviour and universal Judge, the Lord, having a Name which is above every name, before whom every knee must bend, and in whose hand lies the destiny of every creature; He is the One who liveth and was dead, and behold He is alive for evermore and hath the keys of Hades and of death; He is Emmanuel, God with us, and in Him dwelleth all the Fulness of the Godhead bodily; He is the great God and our Saviour Jesus Christ; the bright Morning Star, the true God and Eternal Life, and the I AM.

Some of these names belong to Him as having become Man, and as having died and risen again; others describe what He was before He set the pendulum of time in motion, or ever the world was made—what He is in His own uncreated, unchangeable and eternal Being. To these latter belong "the Word", "the only-begotten Son which is in the bosom of the Father", and "the Son" whom the Father only knows. By these names He is distinguished as to His personality in the Godhead, but being one with the Father and the Holy Ghost in the Godhead, He shares in every title that belongs to God, such as "the blessed and only Potentate, King of kings, and Lord of lords; who only hath immortality, dwelling in light which no man can approach unto; whom no man hath seen or can see: to whom be honour and power everlasting. Amen" (1 Timothy 6:15-16). The Father has decreed "that all men should honour the Son even as they honour the Father" (John 5:23). We do this when we own His equality with the Father, and bow before Him as our God. "He that honoureth not the Son, honoureth not the Father which hath sent Him."

We are to consider the entrance of this august Person into the world and to enquire what manner of birth was His who bears all this glory. That He was born of a woman is not disputed; He was a true and proper Man and not a

## THE MIRACULOUS BIRTH: THE FACT AND THE REASON FOR IT

phantom. Every other man born into the world began to be at his conception, and came into the world as a personality that had had no former existence; but our Lord Jesus Christ was rich before His poverty in Bethlehem; He thought it not robbery to be equal with God before He was found in fashion as a Man; He was the Word before He became flesh; He was God's own Son who was sent in the likeness of sinful flesh, made of a woman, when the fulness of time had come (Galatians 4:4). This glorious pre-existence surely means that the birth of our Lord into this world was not as the birth of any other man that had ever been born. His birth was an incarnation, the coming of a Divine Person into a condition in which He had not been before, to carry out all the will of God and be the Saviour of us men.

His birth was a unique event—the greatest, the most amazing that had ever happened; greater by far than the creation of man at the beginning, and unless our minds are darkened to the true meaning of it, we should certainly expect that it would be brought about in some other way than by the ordinary laws of nature; we feel that a Divine Person coming into manhood must have a supernatural birth, and this feeling is established and confirmed by the Word of God.

We open the New Testament and find on the first page of it the story told in simple language, and in about 250 words. It is a subject on which the imagination might have run riot, as it did in the numerous fables and legends that gathered about it as spirituality declined and superstition advanced in the early centuries of the Christian era; but in this God-breathed account of it, the imaginations of man's mind are excluded, and every sentence of the story bears the imprimatur of God. "Now the birth of Jesus Christ was on this wise: When as His mother Mary was espoused to Joseph, before they came together, she was found with child of the Holy Ghost. Then Joseph her husband, being a just man, and not willing to make her a publick example, was minded to put her away privily. But while he thought on these things, the angel of the Lord appeared unto him in a dream saying, Joseph, thou son of David, fear not to take to thee Mary thy wife: for that which is conceived in her is of the Holy Ghost. And she shall bring forth a son, and thou shalt call His name Jesus; for He shall save His people from their sins."

This is the beginning, the door through which we enter into the New Testament and into the realm of infinite and eternal blessedness that it reveals to our souls. It is the beginning of the full and final revelation of God to man. We cannot advance to the climax and completion of this revelation, if we refuse the beginning of it; we must enter into it by the door or be thieves and robbers of the glory of God. The fulness of time had come, and the voice of the Son spoke and said, "A body hast Thou prepared Me ... Lo, I come (in the volume of the book it is written of Me) to do Thy will, O God" (Hebrews 10:5-7).

It is said that only two of the New Testament writers make mention of the Virgin birth. Well, two witnesses are enough, and at their mouth every word shall be established; but does not this saying, "A body hast Thou prepared Me", give a third witness? It surely involves the miraculous conception; and it proclaims the fact that neither the will of the flesh nor the power of man had any place in it, but that the will and wisdom of God combined to prepare that holy incorruptible body within the womb of the Virgin-mother.

## THE MIRACULOUS BIRTH: THE FACT AND THE REASON FOR IT

### Matthew's Record

There are two accounts of this great event. Matthew's Gospel records the communication to Joseph by the angel, and Luke tells us of the annunciation to Mary. And when we discern the respective characters of these two Gospels and the way the Lord is presented in them, we have no difficulty in seeing how perfect these records are, each in its own place. Matthew unfolds the glory of the Lord as King. His Gospel is "the book of the generation of JESUS CHRIST, THE SON OF DAVID, the Son of Abraham." He came as the Heir to the throne of David and to establish and fulfil all the promises made to Abraham. But here was a difficulty; while Jesus Christ was the long-promised Heir, Joseph stood in the direct line of succession and was the legal heir, as this genealogy proves. And this was recognised by the Lord's messenger when he saluted him as "Joseph, thou son of David." He was an obscure village carpenter, proving the truth of the words of the prophet that the tabernacle of David had fallen down and lay in ruins (Amos 9:11), and yet he showed traits of true royalty according to God, in that he was "a just man" and in his compassion and merciful intention toward the weak, and as he thought, failing woman, and in his trust in the Word of God and obedience to it.

It was right that he should have been addressed by the angel not only because of his own personal concern as to the condition of his espoused wife, but also because of his care for the integrity of the succession to the throne of David. It might appear a foolish and futile thing to have been concerned about the latter, seeing that six centuries had passed since the sceptre had departed from the house of David, but faith holds on to the promises of God, even when human strength has failed and every visible hope has fled; and Joseph was a man of faith. And being a man of faith, he did as he was bidden by the angel of the Lord and took Mary unto him as his wife, without hesitation or further misgiving; and by so doing, he cast the protection of his name about her, and made her first-born Son his Heir—the *legal* Heir to David's throne.

But there was a matter of even greater importance than what was due to Joseph and the integrity of the Royal line and the necessity of Jesus Christ being the legal Heir to the throne; there was God's own integrity and His faithfulness to His Word. And these were made good and revealed in the words, "Now all this was done, that it might be fulfilled which was spoken of the Lord by the prophet, saying, Behold, a virgin shall be with child, and shall bring forth a Son, and they shall call His name Emmanuel, which being interpreted is, God with us." That was the most astonishing prophecy that God ever gave through a prophet's lips; it means, as we hope to show, the intervention of God in a new and personal way for the deliverance of His people; it foretold something that would be outside and apart from all the power of man, and, impossible as it may seem to be to men who have no faith, it was fulfilled when the espoused wife of Joseph brought forth a Son, whose name was called JESUS, the Saviour of His people from their sins.

In that lowly Babe, the Virgin's Son, conceived by the power of the Holy Ghost, the two Testaments are bound together; the hopes of the Old and the faith of the New unite in Him, and we can with exultation take up the prophetic word and join with Israel and say, "Unto us a Child is born, unto us a Son is given; and the government shall be on His shoulder: and His Name shall be called Wonderful, Counsellor, the mighty God, the everlasting Father, the Prince of Peace. Of the increase of His government there shall be no end, upon the throne of David

## THE MIRACULOUS BIRTH: THE FACT AND THE REASON FOR IT

and upon His kingdom, to order it, and to establish it with judgment and justice from henceforth for ever. THE ZEAL OF THE LORD OF HOSTS WILL PERFORM THIS" (Isaiah 9:6-7).

### LUKE'S RECORD

The Gospel of Luke was written to a Gentile believer and has the world in view rather than Israel; consequently there was not the same necessity as in Matthew's Gospel to show that the birth of the Lord was in accordance with the prophecies made in the Old Testament to Israel. In it the Lord is presented as true Man, born of a woman, come in grace to all men, and there was not the same need to give Joseph the prominence that he has in Matthew's Gospel, where the true heirship to David's throne was a vital matter. But there was need that all people to whom "the good tidings of great joy" as to the Saviour, who is Christ the Lord, were brought, should know from whence He came and how, that they might understand and appreciate the fact that His coming was not by the power of man, but entirely of God and in sovereign grace. The annunciation to Mary, a lowly daughter of David's house, and espoused to a working man, brings out this grace in its unsurpassable richness and charm.

Gabriel's message from God to Mary is divided into three parts. *First,* the salutation which proclaims the greatness of the favour that God was to bestow upon her. Unknown and poor though she was, she was chosen by sovereign grace from among all women to be the vessel by whom God would bring about His great purpose. *Second,* there was the revelation of what this purpose was. "Fear not, Mary," said the angel, "for thou hast found favour with God. And, behold, thou shalt conceive in thy womb, and bring forth a Son, and shalt call His name JESUS. He shall be great and shall be called the Son of the Highest: and the Lord God shall give unto Him the throne of His father David: and He shall reign over the house of Jacob for ever, and of His kingdom there shall be no end." He that was to be born to her was to be the Son of David, and to have His father's throne: that she might have understood, seeing she belonged to the house of David, but how could He be JESUS—Jehovah the Saviour? How could He be called the Son of the Highest? The Highest is the title of God in His supremacy over all the earth, and in heaven; the One whose word and ways none may challenge, and who will manifest Himself thus in the coming Millennial Kingdom. How could the Son of her womb have the right to be called His Son? We do not wonder that she asked that question; it was a right and proper question to ask, and it brought out the *third* part of Gabriel's message from God which enlightened her as to how it was to be brought to pass. "The Holy Ghost shall come upon thee, the power of the Highest shall overshadow thee therefore also that holy Thing which shall be born of thee shall be called the Son of God."

This last utterance of the angel "who stands in the presence of God" requires no comment. It most surely drives away all doubt for those who will believe. The birth of the Saviour was miraculous, it was by God's power, it was God's work. Man and his corruptible seed had no part in it; the Son of Mary was holy and undefiled. He was the Son of God. Of this J. N. Darby has written, "It is not here the doctrine of the eternal relationship of Son with the Father. The Gospel of John, the Epistle to the Hebrews and that to the Colossians, establish this precious truth and demonstrate its importance, but here it is that which is born by virtue of the miraculous conception, which on that ground is called the Son of God" [1]. And if unbelief says it is contrary to every law of nature and impossible, faith answers in the words of Gabriel, who knew God's power so well, "with God nothing shall be impossible."

### THE NECESSITY FOR THE VIRGIN BIRTH

The fact that men need a Saviour, a Deliverer, is evident everywhere, and has been all through their history since the fall. And the first promise that one should appear followed swiftly upon Satan's triumph over man in Eden, and it came forth from the mouth of God. "The Seed of the woman", said He to the victorious serpent, "shall bruise thy head and thou shalt bruise His heel." If Adam had been able to recover himself and bruise his tempter and conqueror beneath his feet, God would have stood aside and let him do it, but there could be no hope from him or from any that he could beget. If he had fallen a prey to Satan's subtlety when he stood erect in the plenitude of his powers, how could he by any means recover what he had lost now that he was defeated and fettered by Satan, and lying under the sentence of death by God's just decree? All his progeny were powerless like himself. "By one man sin entered into the world and death by sin, and death passed upon all men for that all have sinned" (Romans 5:12). The hope was not in Adam but in the woman's Seed. It was He, whoever He might be, who was to destroy the great destroyer of our frail and fallen race, and deliver us from his power. The New Testament tells us plainly who He is. "For this purpose", says 1 John 3:8, "was THE SON OF GOD manifested, that He might destroy the works of the devil." And Hebrews 2:15 tells us that THE SON—in whom God has spoken in these last days—because "the children were partakers of flesh and blood, also Himself likewise took part of the same; that through death, He might destroy him that had the power of death, that is, the devil; and deliver them who through fear of death were all their lifetime subject to bondage." It is plain from these Scriptures that the Seed of the woman is the Son of God, and we are told that "all the promises of God in Him are yea and in Him Amen."

The first promise prepares us for the Virgin birth and we are not surprised to read, "Behold, a virgin shall conceive and bear a Son, and shall call His name Emmanuel." And if unbelief persists in declaring that to be impossible, faith answers, Yes, with men it is impossible; and that is the great and solemn fact that this God-given sign throws into prominence, it is the very lesson that God would teach by the manner of His intervention. Men are unable to save themselves and unable to find amongst even the best of Adam's fallen children one man who can redeem his brother, or give the just ransom for him. Every man needs a Saviour for himself, and because of that, God has stepped in and has provided the Man—the Kinsman-Redeemer, but He has done it in a way that humbles the pride of man and sets him aside. "A virgin shall conceive and bear a son." The Virgin's Son would owe nothing to man; His very presence in the world would be independent of man. His coming into the world would be God's work. It would be God's intervention in miraculous power and sovereign mercy—the salvation of the Lord. So we read that in due time, Mary brought forth her firstborn Son and "wrapped Him in swaddling clothes and laid Him in a manger; because there was no room for them in the inn." Thus came Emmanuel, apart from all the power of men and outside the abodes of men, for not only could not men produce the Deliverer, but they did not want Him when He came.

## THE MIRACULOUS BIRTH: THE FACT AND THE REASON FOR IT

### Does it Matter?

Like produces like. This is one of the fundamental laws of nature as established by God. It is stamped upon the Creation chapter—fish, fowl, and flesh were all ordained to bring forth each "after his kind". And man could do no other than this. "Adam", we read, "begat a son in his own likeness, after his own image" (Genesis 5:3). And so it has been throughout all the generations of men. Sinful men beget sinful children. Therefore it is written, "They go astray as soon as they are born, speaking lies" (Psalm 58:3), and "all we like sheep have gone astray" (Isaiah 53:6), and "All have sinned and come short of the glory of God" (Romans 3:23). In the great penitential Psalm, David confesses, "Behold, I was shapen in iniquity; and in sin did my mother conceive me" (Psalm 51:5), which simply means, "I have come of a sinful stock, my very nature is sinful", and this is true of every man born into the world. Does it matter then or does it not, how the Lord was born into this world? Had He come by natural generation, would He not have been as every other man? To deny the Virgin birth is to deny His pre-existence in the Godhead, and to deny the holiness of His Manhood, and to rob mankind of the one and only Saviour.

It is said that nothing is based upon this great truth in the New Testament. But everything is based upon it; it is the foundation of everything that follows. I stress the fact that it meets us on the first page of the New Testament, that it is the door through which we enter into the full revelation of God. Apart from it, we have no intervention of God for His own glory and our salvation; Jesus is not the great I AM, but a mere man like the rest of men, and we have no sinless Saviour. How, apart from the miraculous conception and the Virgin birth, could the Lord have said, "I know whence I came ... I proceeded forth and came from God ... Verily, verily I say unto you, before Abraham was, I am" (John 8); or how could Peter have applied to Him the words of the Psalm, "Thou wilt not suffer Thine Holy One to see corruption" (Acts 2:27): or the Apostles have spoken of Him as God's Holy Child, Jesus (4:30). Or how could Paul have spoken of Him as "Christ who is over all, God blessed for ever" (Romans 9:5), or as "the Second Man, the Lord out of heaven" (1 Corinthians 15:47); or how could John have insisted with such persistence on the fact that Jesus is the Son of God and the great object of faith, the true God and Eternal Life?

For ourselves, we linger with the shepherds as they gather round the Babe in the manger; we press into the house with the Magi from the East and worship the young Child with them. We own Him to be truly Man—sinless and holy; but more, for we confess Him, as did Thomas, when he saw His wounded hands and side after He had risen from the dead, OUR LORD AND OUR GOD. And we say as we consider the manner of God's intervention for His glory and our eternal blessing, "O the depth of the riches both of the wisdom and the knowledge of God! How unsearchable are His judgments, and His ways past finding out! For who hath known the mind of the Lord? or who hath been His counsellor? or who hath first given to Him, and it shall be recompensed to Him again? For of Him, and through Him, and to Him are all things; to whom be glory for ever. Amen" (Romans 11:33-36).

# The Deity of the Lord Jesus
## The Necessity for It

## CONCERNING HIMSELF

"I, even I, am the Lord, and beside Me there is no Saviour. ... I, even I, am He that blotteth out thy transgressions for Mine own sake, and will not remember thy sins. ... Look unto Me, and be ye saved, all the ends of the earth: for I am God, and there is none else."—Isaiah 43:11, 25; 45:22.

# Chapter 2
# The Deity of the Lord Jesus

## THE NECESSITY FOR IT

We can understand the envy with which the kings of Egypt would view the rise and progress of Israel. They had held that nation as slaves for many generations but had been compelled by the power of Jehovah to release them, and had seen Jerusalem become the most magnificent and wealthiest city on earth under the rule of David and Solomon. Small wonder that at the first evidence of weakness Shishak came up against that city with a great army and pillaged the Temple and the king's house, and took away the priceless treasure of them, including the shields of gold that Solomon had made. Then Rehoboam, that feeble and foolish son of a great father, does not appear to have put up any resistance; he let the glory of the city go without protest. What did it matter? He could substitute brass for gold, and brass looks like gold, almost; peace seemed cheap at the price. And so it was when he went up to the house of the Lord, brazen shields went up before him instead of shields of fine gold, and when his religious duties were done they were committed to the guard for safe keeping as though they were the real thing (1 Kings 14).

What the king of Egypt did to Jerusalem, the devil, who is the god and prince of the world, has done for Christendom. For ages he had held mankind in darkness and bondage, but deliverance came at the advent of the Lord Jesus, who lived among men and died and rose again. Then "God was manifest in the flesh, justified in the Spirit, seen of angels, preached unto the Gentiles, believed on in the world, received up into glory." Multitudes were delivered from the kingdom of darkness and translated into the kingdom of the Son of the Father's love, and there was established on earth the kingdom of heaven which was enriched by heavenly treasure: the pure gold of God's truth concerning His Son, Jesus Christ our Lord.

But with the decline of living faith and the rise of profession without reality in these modern days, the devil has seen and seized his opportunity, and has laid his envious and ruthless hands upon these treasures and has robbed an indifferent and faithless church of its shields of gold. He could not have done it if there had not been traitors within who were pledged to hold and fight for these treasures—"the Faith once for all delivered to the saints." They have been his allies in this.

The truth as to the person of the Lord is the finest of the gold of our faith; what He is in His own eternal Being gives character to it all. It is declared in the following great texts: "God was manifest in the flesh", not, "Jesus was a manifestation of God", as some say, but that He is Himself, in His own person, God. "In the beginning was the Word, and the Word was with God, and the Word was God. The same was in the beginning with God ... and the Word was made flesh, and dwelt among us (and we beheld His glory, the glory as of the only-begotten of the Father), full of grace and truth" (John 1:1-14). But this fine gold has been surrendered by many leaders in Christendom, who ought to have defended it to the death. They have surrendered it with other priceless treasures for popularity with the world and in fear of "modern scholarship". They seem to be well pleased to let these great truths go, for their insubject minds prefer their own investigations to God's revelation, and man's effort to uplift himself is more to them than God's intervention for his redemption and they have seized the opportunity to substitute their own base brass for God's fine gold. A Christ of their imagination is more to their liking than the Christ of God, a Christ who is stripped of the glory of His eternal Deity, and being stripped of that supreme glory is stripped of every other glory that could be acceptable to God and of use to men. And they think that they are the gainers by the change. "We are rich and increased with goods," they boast, "and have need of nothing", and they know not that "they are wretched and miserable and poor and blind and naked" and need to turn again to our Sovereign Lord and buy of Him gold tried in the fire that they may be rich (Revelation 3:17-18).

The pretence of approach to God is kept up, but the brazen shields go before them instead of shields of gold, and God will not have their counterfeits. "I am the way, the truth and the life: no man cometh unto the Father but by Me" (John 14:6), are our Lord's own words, and they are recorded for us in that Gospel which reveals to us the glory of His divine and eternal Being, which indeed is not absent from any part of Scripture; and nothing less than this will do for God. The brazen imitation may suit and fascinate men, but it is an abomination to God, nothing but the pure gold can He accept, and in vain is their worship of Him as long as they teach the doctrines and opinions of men for the gospel of God concerning His Son, Jesus Christ our Lord.

And nothing but the pure gold of this gospel will satisfy the soul of a man when he is fully awakened to his deep need. When the light of God streams into his conscience and he sees the exceeding sinfulness of his sin, and the greatness of his peril and how far his sin has removed him from God, he will spurn the brass of man's imagination as a mockery and a sham, and confess that there can be for him no salvation in any other Name, but the Name of JESUS—Jehovah the Saviour. As to this, the late Handley Moule wrote, "The human soul, once fully awakened to its needs, to its mysterious greatness and to its mysterious but awfully real sinfulness, can find rest only in the Saviour, who is, in equal truth, one with man and one with God. Such a Saviour bridges as with living adamant the gulf of doom and sin which severs creature from Maker. A saviour who is not quite God is a bridge broken at the farther end" [2].

It is here I would begin; before endeavouring to show that all Scripture bears witness to the fact that Jesus is the eternal Word, "The Christ, who is over all, God blessed for ever", I would urge the necessity for it. It is a necessity to God, if He is to be known by His creature, and to find His delights in the sons of men, redeemed from all iniquity and purified unto Himself as a peculiar people, zealous of good works; it is a necessity to man if he is ever to know God as his God, to be forgiven, and at peace, and find his soul's everlasting satisfaction in Him. The human soul would grope in vain for light if it were not so; it would cry out hopelessly in its misery, for there would be none to help; there would be "neither voice, nor any to answer, nor any that regarded", as it was when the

## THE DEITY OF THE LORD JESUS: THE NECESSITY FOR IT

prophets of Baal cried all the day long to their false god (1 Kings 18: 29). We should be a lost race, wandering stars cut off from our central Sun without hope of restoration to our true orbit and with no outlook but the blackness of darkness for ever, if Jesus were not God: "the only begotten Son which is in the bosom of the Father."

Consider the cry that broke out of the awakened soul of that pagan jailor at Philippi, "Sirs, what must I do to be saved?" (Acts 16:30). What answer could satisfy that bewildered man, trembling on the brink of a lost eternity? There was but one answer that could satisfy him. Suppose instead of that one and only answer Paul had said, "Believe in Adam, or Abraham, or Moses, or John the Baptist." What a mocker of the man's misery he would have been; or suppose he had said, for he was a greater man than them all, "Believe on me and thou shalt be saved." Would not the soul and conscience of the jailor have revolted against the outrage and have turned from him as a blasphemer and an impostor? But how fitting, how satisfying was the answer that he did give, "Believe on the Lord Jesus Christ and thou shalt be saved, and thy house." The whole gospel of God was involved in that answer; it put that seeking sinner into vital contact with Him who of old had said, "Look unto Me, and be ye saved, all the ends of the earth: for I am God, and there is none beside Me" (Isaiah 45:22), it satisfied him, for it gave him a perfect, because a divine Saviour.

The necessity for the Word to become flesh did not arise only when that great event took place, it was there from the beginning when sin entered into the world. The patriarch Job felt the necessity and voiced it in memorable words when he said, as he searched for a way by which a man could be just with God: "He is not a man as I am, that I should answer Him, and we should come together in judgment. Neither is there any daysman betwixt us, that might lay his hand upon us both. Let Him take away His rod from me, and let not His fear terrify me: then would I speak, and not fear Him; but it is not so with me" (Job 9:32-35). It is not difficult to interpret what his feelings were, for they are the feelings of all who have been awakened by God's Spirit to their need. He said in effect: "I know that I have sinned against Him, and if He were a man as I am, I could, having the feelings of a man, understand how I have offended Him; I could go to Him and make restitution for the wrong I have done to Him and so be at peace. But He is not a man as I am, and I cannot measure the demands of His justice against me. The gulf between us is unmeasurable from my side; He is almighty, holy and just, and I am weak, sinful and unholy, and there is no one that I know of to stand betwixt us, who could speak from Him to me, and from me to Him." See how accurately his awakened conscience had gauged the situation: he desired one who could stand betwixt God, infinitely holy and just, and the sinner, guilty and afraid, and put his hand upon them both: He must be equal to God and equal to men. And says Job, "I do not know such a one. I have felt the need for Him, I have longed for Him and sought for Him but I have not found Him." And Job, be it noted, who expressed his soul's deep longing in these words, was the man who came nearer to perfection than any man of his day; and if he was hopeless and despairing because he had no Daysman, it is plain that the Daysman, the Mediator, could not arise from among men such as he was. If He is to come at all He must come from above, and when He comes, He must be able to put His hand upon God: He must be God's equal; pure as God is pure, holy as God is holy, great as God is great: no one less could intervene, or be of any use in this supreme matter to Job or to any other man. Yet He must come low enough to put His hand upon men. He must pass by angels and be one of us, yet sinless, or His touch would defile the throne of God and be unavailing for us. He must represent God and yet be able to identify Himself with us, or He could not take up our vast indebtedness and speak for us. *He must be God and man.*

Man's extremity is God's opportunity, and the One whom Job could not find on earth has come from heaven, and Jesus, the Virgin's Son, is Emmanuel: God With Us. Being God, He knew according to God's perfect estimate what the effect to the universe of man's sin was. He knew how the majesty of God was challenged by man's disregard of His will, and what the demands of the eternal throne were in regard to the violation of its just decrees. He knew how man's pride and self will had made him the lawful captive of Satan, and how great was the gulf that separated him from his God, and how powerless he was to right the wrong. He knew the penalty that had to be paid and the work that had to be done, and knowing all this He came, saying, "A body hast Thou prepared Me ... Lo, I come (in the volume of the book it is written of Me) to do Thy will, O God" (Hebrews 10:5-7). He became the Son of Man, that He might stand in the place of men, and be lifted up as their substitute and representative and meet the bill of their indebtedness. This involved Him in all the sorrows of Calvary, and there "He gave Himself a ransom for all." If He had not become man He could not have died, if He had not been God His death would have been without value, but now His death accomplished and the ransom paid, He is "the one Mediator between God and men, the Man Christ Jesus" (1 Timothy 2:5).

He stooped from His eternal glory and was made in the likeness of men, and being found in fashion as a man He put His hand upon us, degraded though we were, and He did it tenderly, graciously so that we are not afraid. He is full of grace and truth and there is no terror for us in His hand; we do not shrink from Him, for He has touched us with the hand of a man, yet He was never less than God, and God has touched us in Him. He has put one hand upon us and the other He has placed upon the throne of God. With the one hand He has offered the fullest satisfaction to every righteous claim of God, and with the other He bestows fulness of grace upon men. He brings us to God and gives us a place in His presence without fear, and in everlasting peace, a place established upon an infallible and immovable foundation of divine righteousness laid down by Him who is God and Man in His own blessed person.

But if the necessity on man's side was great, it was even greater on God's side; the fulfilment of His purposes and the revelation of the deep love of His heart towards men as well as the glory of His Name all depend upon the Deity of the Lord Jesus. How could God reveal Himself to men who were cut off from Him by their sins? How could He win their hearts from their fear and hatred of Him and deliver them from the darkness in which they groped? How could men love God if they did not know Him, and how could they know Him, since no man hath seen God at any time unless the only-begotten Son which is in His bosom came forth to declare Him? It was certainly necessary that these things should be done if ever that great word was to be fulfilled, "And I heard a great voice out of heaven saying, Behold the tabernacle of God is with men, and He will dwell with them, and they shall be His people, and God Himself shall be with them, and be their God. And God shall wipe away all tears from their eyes; and there shall be no more death, neither sorrow, nor crying, neither shall there be any more pain, for the former things are passed away" (Revelation 21:3-4).

Before all this could be an accomplished fact the sin of the world must be borne away, and who could do that? It is recorded that, "John (the Baptist) seeth Jesus coming unto him, and saith, Behold the Lamb of God, which taketh away the sin of the world" (John 1:29). We are familiar with the words, so familiar that we are but lightly impressed with their immensity and meaning. "The sin of the world"! Think of it! Think of the sin of one city, what man could take that away? or of one street in a city, or of one house in that street, or of one man in that house? Could any man take away his own sin and stand before God, "holy and without blame before Him in love"? for nothing less than that will suit Him. The questions have only to be asked to prove to all who are not wilfully blind that this work could only lie in the hands of the eternal God. Yet as John saw that lowly Stranger from Nazareth moving towards him among the multitudes of Israel, he proclaimed Him to be the Taker-away of the sin of the world, and in that word he proclaimed His Godhead power and worth. No wonder that he was compelled to add, "This is He of whom I said, After me cometh a man which is preferred before me: for He was before me."

That which is written in Revelation 21 shall come to pass, for "the words are true and faithful" (verse 5). The same voice that cried, "It is finished" on the cross at Golgotha shall be heard saying "It is done", and God shall rest with the multitude of His redeemed sons in His own love that has been declared by the Son, and shall be all and in all to them for ever. Meanwhile He declares, "I am Alpha and Omega, the beginning and the end. I will give unto him that is athirst of *the fountain* of the water of life." God Himself is the Fountain, and the thirst of the human soul can only be assuaged and satisfied with God, and God is fully revealed to us in Jesus. For "God was manifest in the flesh, justified in the Spirit, seen of angels, preached unto the Gentiles, believed on in the world, received up into glory" (1 Timothy 3:16).

# The Deity of the Lord Jesus
## IN THE OPENING OF THE NEW TESTAMENT

Here, then, is that which the Spirit of God sets before us: Jesus, the Son of David, conceived by the power of the Holy Ghost; Jehovah, the Saviour, to deliver Israel from their sins; God with us: who could comprehend or fathom the mystery of His nature in whom all these things combined? His life, in fact, as we shall see, displays the obedience of the perfect Man, and the perfection and the power of God.—J. N. DARBY [3].

# Chapter 3
# The Deity of the Lord Jesus

## IN THE OPENING OF THE NEW TESTAMENT

It was not the work of earlier writers of the New Testament to prove that the Lord Jesus Christ is God. To them this great truth was not a matter of question or debate, it was their whole faith, and the standpoint from which they made their inspired-by-the-Holy-Spirit records. It has been said that just as the golden threads were inextricably woven with the blue and purple and scarlet and fine linen of the High Priest's ephod and girdle (Exodus 18) so is the Deity of Christ woven into all that these men wrote; and that is true, yet the type is feeble and inadequate, as all material types of what is infinite must be. The Deity of Christ is more than interwoven into the Gospel records, it is the warp upon which all that is recorded in them is wrought; it is the root out of which all truth grows; it is the fountain from which all blessing flows. If it could be torn from these four Gospels they would be meaningless shreds, and the glorious faith of the Son of God would be compelled to take its place along with other vain, worldly philosophies, having some interest perhaps to scholars, but void of all saving value for sinners. Those who reject it, reject the only hope, the only way of deliverance for men, for all Scripture shows that if men were to be saved, God must come down to them to do it, and also, if God does come down to men, He must come as their Saviour.

And it is with this that the New Testament opens. Upon the first page of it, in our Authorised Version, the Name of JESUS appears in capital letters, and it gives us the title and the great subject of the Book. That Name means Saviour, and He had come to save. The New Testament is the Book of God's salvation, and it shows us that God Himself is the Saviour, and He only. He might delegate great works to His angel-servants, and speak in divers ways to men by His prophets, but this work of salvation He must undertake Himself, or it would never be done.

Let us now consider this, "Fear not", said the angel of the Lord to Joseph, "to take unto thee Mary thy wife: for that which is conceived in her is of the Holy Ghost. And she shall bring forth a son, and thou shalt call His name JESUS: for He shall save His people from their sins" (Matthew 1:20-21). He did not say that He would save sinners, Jew and Gentile, though that is most blessedly true, and comes fully to light as the truth unfolds, but to "save His people". His people were Israel, and they were in view in the angel's announcement, and the fulfilment of the word of God by His prophets to them. They were Jehovah's people, a people chosen of God as His own peculiar possession, even though they had departed far from Him. Their sins had separated them from Him, but He would not abandon His rights in them. He could not if He was to be faithful to His word and promise. He must undertake their salvation. And Jesus was to appear to do this, because, as the angel said, these people chosen of God were *His* PEOPLE.

## THE DEITY OF THE LORD JESUS:
## IN THE OPENING OF THE NEW TESTAMENT

There are many Old Testament passages addressed to Israel which bind up their salvation with God's personal intervention on their behalf and that prove conclusively that He only could save them. I will quote a few of them, "I am the Lord thy God, the Holy One of Israel, thy Saviour" (Isaiah 43:3). "I, even I, am the Lord, and beside Me there is no Saviour" (43:11). "There is no God else beside Me, a just God and a Saviour" (45:21). "All flesh shall know that I the Lord am thy Saviour, and thy Redeemer, the mighty One of Jacob" (49:26). "I am the Lord thy God from the land of Egypt, and thou shalt know no god but Me; for there is no Saviour beside Me" (Hosea 13:4). The name Jesus carries divine glory with it; that it means Jehovah the Saviour; and it is certainly clear from these great texts that none but God could be the Saviour, and if any others pretended to be able to do this, their pretence only proved them to be thieves and robbers (John 10), but of Jesus, the angel said, "He shall save His people from their sins." Then who else could He be but God?

### THE FIRST QUOTATION FROM THE PROPHETS

As we apprehend the force and meaning of the words of the angel of the Lord to Joseph we are prepared for the statement that follows, "Now this was done, that it might be fulfilled which was spoken of the Lord by the prophet saying, Behold, a virgin shall be with child, and shall bring forth a son, and they shall call His name Emmanuel, which being interpreted is, God with us" (Matthew 1:22-23). When Mary brought forth her firstborn Son the Saviour-Messiah had entered the world, He who had said to Moses, "I AM THAT I AM: Thus shalt thou say unto the children of Israel I AM hath sent me to you" (Exodus 3:14), was not now sending a servant with a message but He had appeared Himself to be their

Saviour. This mystery of God-incarnate must ever baffle all intellectual investigation, but it does not stumble faith; for faith expects that God will perform His word. If He had spoken of this by the prophet, what He had said must come to pass. And faith knows that when God moves He moves in a way worthy of Himself. He confounds the wise and the proud and the mighty by that which is apparently weak and of no account. It was even so in this matter. He came into manhood and in great humility, not to condemn and consume a sinful people, but to offer Himself to them as their Saviour and Lord.

### The Second Quotation from the Prophets

The coming of the wise men from the East to enquire where He was who was born King of the Jews, gave Jerusalem the opportunity of not only beholding its King but of seeing its God manifest in flesh. The chief men of the city were gathered together by Herod, the Idumean usurper, and they showed that they were well acquainted with the Scriptures that spoke of His birth. But in citing Micah 5:2, why did they omit that part of it that declares His eternal Being and activities? The omission seems to indicate that they had no desire for a close acquaintance with their God, the idea was not acceptable to them; an alien tyrant seems to have been more to their minds than Jehovah their Saviour. But the prophecy which they quoted not only foretold the place of His birth and the dignity of His office, but the glory of His Person. Micah wrote, "They shall smite the Judge of Israel with a rod upon the cheek"—an extraordinary prophecy; but actually fulfilled when they took the reed that they had put in His right hand as a mock sceptre and smote Him on the head (Matthew 27:30)—"But thou Bethlehem Ephratah, though thou be little among the thousands of Judah, yet out of thee shall He come forth unto Me that

## THE DEITY OF THE LORD JESUS: IN THE OPENING OF THE NEW TESTAMENT

is to be ruler in Israel; *whose goings forth have been from of old, from everlasting (or the days of eternity)*" (Micah 5:1-2).

Who could have conceived this strange thing, that He whose goings forth were from eternity, who in divine, creative energy had cast the stars before Him as a golden pathway for His glorious feet, should have come forth in obscure Bethlehem, born of an obscure virgin-mother, in all the apparent weakness of human babehood, to be the Servant of the Godhead and to tread the filthy streets of those eastern cities in His search for the diseased and distressed and devil-possessed, and to go forth at last bearing His cross to Golgotha to save His people from their sins? What goings forth were these! Yet these were the ways of divine love, made known in the Son of Man, who came not to be ministered unto but to minister and to give His life a ransom for many. It was the only way if God was to be known as the Saviour, and if Jesus was to make good His title to that glorious Name.

### THE THIRD QUOTATION FROM THE PROPHETS

Passing over other quotations from the prophets that do not bear on our subject we come to Matthew chapter 3. John the Baptist was a man full of the Holy Spirit, and by the guidance and power of the Spirit he bore testimony to Jesus. He refused to talk of himself; his mission was to "prepare the way of the LORD", according to the prophecy of Isaiah (40:3). And of Him whose forerunner he was, he said, "He that cometh after me is mightier than I, whose shoes I am not worthy to bear, He shall baptise you with the Holy Ghost and with fire: whose fan is in His hand and He will throughly purge His floor, and gather His wheat into the garner, but He will burn up the chaff with unquenchable fire" (Matthew 3:11-12). With the Lord close upon his heels, this faithful Forerunner declared his own limitations; he could baptise the people with water; he could bring them down into that which signified death and no more; but at the same time he proclaimed the might of his Lord. He would lift them into the sphere of life and endue them with the power and intelligence that belonged to that life, or—dread alternative—baptise them with fire. He would gather His wheat into the garner and burn the chaff with unquenchable fire.

Israel was His floor, and He the Lord would discriminate between His wheat and the chaff. Who but *the Lord* could do this? It is written, "The Lord knoweth them that are His" (2 Timothy 2:19). He had come in grace, the Lord in whom is salvation, but He had come to a recalcitrant nation, a remnant only of which would receive Him; and since He is a *just God* as well as a Saviour, His judgment must fall on the rebellious. "For the day cometh, that shall burn as an oven; and all the proud, yea, all that do wickedly shall be stubble: and the day that cometh shall burn them up saith the Lord of hosts, that it shall leave them neither root nor branch" (Malachi 4:1). "The Father ... hath committed all judgment to the Son: that all men should honour the Son, even as they honour the Father" (John 5:22-23). "What a fact of immeasurable greatness was the presence of the Lord God in the midst of His people, in the Person of Him who, although He was doubtless to be the fulfilment of all the promises, was necessarily, though rejected, the Judge of all the evil existing among His people" (J. N. Darby [4]).

### THE FOURTH QUOTATION FROM THE PROPHETS

The next quotation from the prophets which has a definite bearing on our subject is in Matthew chapter 4. John had been cast into prison. He had been a burning and a shining light in the darkness, but as the stars fade away

## THE DEITY OF THE LORD JESUS:
### IN THE OPENING OF THE NEW TESTAMENT

when the sun rises, so he passed out of sight that all eyes might be fixed upon the One who was greater than he; "that it might be fulfilled which was spoken by Esaias the prophet, saying, The land of Zabulon, and the land of Nephthalim, by the way of the sea, beyond Jordan, Galilee of the Gentiles: the people which sat in darkness saw a great light; and to them which sat in the region of the shadow of death light is sprung up" (Matthew 4:14-16). The quotation is from the 9th chapter of the prophecy and it declares the greatness of the One in whom this great light shone, and we must not fail to notice this. "Unto us", says the prophet, "a child is born, unto us a son is given: and the government shall be on His shoulder: and His Name shall be called Wonderful, Counsellor, The Mighty God, the Father of Eternity, the Prince of Peace. Of the increase of His government and peace there shall be no end, upon the throne of David, and upon His Kingdom to order it and to establish it with judgment and with justice from henceforth even for ever. The zeal of the Lord of hosts will perform this" (Isaiah 9:6-7).

How great are the glories of this five-fold name! too bright indeed for mortal eyes, if it were not in Jesus that they shine, but in Him they reach us as softly and sweetly as the dawn, "Unto us *a child is born, unto us a son is given.*" Here is meekness, gentleness and love. We are not afraid of a babe; we do not shrink in terror from a son. "Fear not," said the angel to the Shepherds, "for behold, I bring you tidings of great joy, which shall be to all people. For unto you is born this day in the city of David a Saviour, which is Christ the Lord. And this shall be a sign unto you: Ye shall find the babe wrapped in swaddling clothes lying in a manger" (Luke 2:10-12). And His Name—the name of that Babe upon whom the Shepherds looked with wonder and whom the wise men worshipped—has a five-fold glory. Can we discern it in the Gospels? I think we can, indeed it pervades them and diffuses its fragrance from every page of them.

His name shall be called WONDERFUL. The devil owned it when he was compelled to leave Him, having utterly failed to allure Him from the path of righteousness (Matthew 4:11). The people confessed it when they were astonished at His doctrine (7:28); the soldiers who were sent to take Him were compelled to own it when they said, "Never man spake like this Man" (John 7:46); the people confessed it again when they said, "He hath done all things well" (Mark 7:37); His disciples felt it when they asked, "What manner of man is this?" (Matthew 8:27); the devils were forced to the confession of it when they said, "What have we to do with Thee, Jesus of Nazareth?" (Luke 4:34; Matthew 8:29); and the Father proclaimed it when from the excellent glory He said, "Thou art My Son, (even) the Beloved, in whom I greatly delight."

COUNSELLOR. "Learn of Me," He said, "for I am meek and lowly in heart, and ye shall find rest to your souls" (Matthew 11:29), and "Whosoever heareth these sayings of Mine, and doeth them, I will liken him unto a wise man, which built his house upon a rock, and the floods came, and the winds blew, and beat upon that house: and it fell not: for it was founded upon a rock" (7:24-25).

THE MIGHTY GOD. This is the name of God as the Omnipotent One, the mighty EL, the Most High, possessor of heaven and earth, Who disposes of men as He will, and is the strength and refuge of those that trust in Him. This is the central glory of the five-fold Name and it shone from the lowly Nazarene when He stilled the storm on the midnight sea (8:26); thrust back and controlled the power of death (9:18, 25); multiplied the loaves and fishes to satisfy the hungry crowds (14:19); claimed the undivided allegiance of the hearts of men (4:18-22; 19:21); forgave the sins of those that sought Him (9:2); and said, "Come unto Me, all ye that labour and are heavy laden, and I will give you rest" (11:28).

THE FATHER OF ETERNITY. Our minds can travel back through the ages of time, but they halt at the frontiers of eternity; yet this fourth beam of this all-glorious Name carries us into eternity whether we will or not, and tells us that every age of it proceeded from Him, and that He controls them with all their issues. If I may be permitted to go outside this Gospel of Matthew I will quote from Colossians 1, where it is said of "*The Son of the Father's love*" (verse 13), "for by Him were all things created, that are in heaven, and that are in earth, visible and invisible, whether they be thrones, or dominions, or principalities, or powers: all things were created by Him, and for Him; and He is before all things, and by Him all things consist" (verses 16-17). And turning back to our Gospel I read of this Creator-Son, "No man knoweth the Son but the Father" (Matthew 11:27), and there shines a beam too bright for creature eye, a glory that no man hath seen or can see.

THE PRINCE OF PEACE. There is not much said about peace in Matthew's Gospel—it belongs more to Luke's and the latter part of John's—but the reason is not far to seek. As the Prince of Peace, He sent forth His messengers preaching peace in every house into which they went, but the people were not worthy of that peace, for they rejected the Prince of it, and the peace they would not have returned to those who carried it (10:13), and the Prince of Peace had to say in view of this stubbornness and blindness, "Think not that I am come to send peace on earth: I came not to send peace but a sword" (10:34). Nevertheless He was the Prince of Peace, and Peter proclaimed this when He told the first Gentiles that ever heard the gospel, "The word which God sent unto the children of Israel, preaching peace by Jesus Christ: (He is Lord of all)" (Acts 10:36). And all who owned His Lordship entered into peace then as they also do even unto this day.

The glory shone in vain for Israel then, for they stumbled at the lowliness of their great Messiah; but the day is surely coming when He will dispel their darkness, and lift the veil that covers them and open their wondering eyes and they shall say in that day, "Lo, this is our God; we have waited for Him, and He will save us: this is the Lord; we have waited for Him, we will be glad and rejoice in His salvation" (Isaiah 25:9). Then of the increase of His government and peace there shall be no end, and He will establish His kingdom with judgment and justice for ever. And He will swallow up death in victory and wipe away tears from off all faces, for He is the Saviour of His people, JEHOVAH-JESUS.

Thus we see Him in the early chapters of Matthew, who is the Son in the glorious Trinity (Matthew 28:19), co-equal with the Father and the Holy Ghost, enter into the world as man, yet Emmanuel, to be the Saviour of His people, and their Ruler, who was not a child of days, but the Lord of Eternity; and their all-discerning and righteous Judge, and the One who will drive before His victorious feet all darkness and the power of death and fill His kingdom and the whole earth with the light of the knowledge of God which shines even now in His face for all who believe.

# The Sinlessness of the Lord Jesus
## Why it Must Be

## CONCERNING HIMSELF

Never once did He confess sin; never once asked for pardon, though He enjoined both upon all others. Indeed, for all others this returning as prodigal, humble and repentant, was the one way that He set forth to the peace and rest of the Father's forgiveness. Yet He never gave a hint, He never breathed a prayer, that implied that He needed this. He challenged His enemies to convince Him of sin. He declared positively that He did always the things that pleased His Father. He had power on earth to forgive sin, but needed no forgiveness Himself.—ADAPTED.

# Chapter 4
# The Sinlessness of the Lord Jesus

## WHY IT MUST BE

Three words are given in Scripture to define sin; they are brought together in Exodus 34:7, Psalm 32 and Psalm 51—they are *transgression, iniquity* and *sin*. These words are not mere synonyms that could displace one another and nothing be lost, for each has its own terrible meaning. TRANSGRESSION is revolt from, it means a tearing of oneself away. God has declared His will for men, but they prefer their own wills, and in pursuit of their own wills they tear themselves away from God. INIQUITY means twisted, crooked, perverse. God has laid down a road for the feet of men to tread, and that road is as straight as His everlasting sceptre, but men have made for themselves crooked ways (Isaiah 59:8); they are a crooked and perverse generation (Philippians 2:15). SIN means missing the mark. God has set up His mark, the end at which every man should aim. God Himself should be the end and aim of every man's life, but every man has substituted self for God, and set up his own mark to displace God's; and has missed the very mark and purpose of his existence. Along with sin in this threefold character goes GUILE; it permeates the life of every man who has not been honest before God. His effort is to appear different to what he knows himself to be, to cover up and hide his sinfulness and even to imagine that he can deceive God Himself as to it. Then the New Testament gives us a striking definition of sin in 1 John 3:4, where we should read, "for sin is lawlessness", and that covers all that sin is; it is not a mere yielding to the sudden and capricious impulses of our nature, but the determination that lies deep in a man's will, though perhaps seldom expressed, to go his own way and be independent of God.

As we consider what sin is as it is defined for us in the Scriptures, we are conscious that we must plead guilty before God to transgression and iniquity and sin, and confess that it is not only in practice that we are sinners, but that we are sinners in our very nature; that what we have done springs out of what we are; the fruit reveals the nature of the root. But we are equally conscious that in this respect our Lord stands out in complete contrast to all that we are; our minds recoil from even the suggestion that there was sin in Him; our spiritual instinct tells us that He was not as we are, that He would be of no use to us if He had been, and we find that these instincts are confirmed by the plainest possible statements in the Word of God.

The flesh and blood that He took was wholly apart from sin. His body was a holy body prepared for Him by God. As a man He was "holy, harmless and undefiled". He was as holy in His manhood nature and life amid the sordidness and sin of the world as He was in the beginning, when by His divine power and glory He created the heavens and the earth. This holy manhood could not have been apart from the miraculous birth. In no other way than that supernatural way could the everlasting Word have come in flesh. Hence in announcing His birth to the Virgin-mother, the angel of the Lord declared, "That *holy Thing* that shall be born of thee, shall be called the Son of God" (Luke 1:35). And from the moment that the Holy Ghost came upon the most blessed of all women, and the power of the Highest overshadowed her, her Firstborn Son was wholly for God; His own words were, "Thou art He that took Me out of the womb; Thou didst make Me hope when I was upon my mother's breasts" (Psalm 22:9).

Heaven and earth and even the nether regions confessed His holiness; God and men and demons bore witness to it. The Holy Ghost descended upon Him at His baptism, not as a burning flame, but as a dove, indicating surely that there was nothing in Him that was obnoxious to the holiness of God's Spirit, but everything in absolute harmony there with Him; and the Father declared that His eye had searched, and found only that in Him that delighted Him. At the very beginning of His public service to God and men, the demons recognised Him and confessed Him as God's holy One (Mark 1:24), and His Apostles, by the inspiration of the Holy Ghost, and in the full light of His life and death and resurrection and ascension to glory, bore witness again and again to this essential fact of our Faith; this fact apart from which our Faith is a delusion and a lie.

### THE SINLESS SACRIFICE FOR SIN

It stands out in the Epistles as a thing to be noted and cherished, that when the question of sin and the sufferings and death of the Lord Jesus as our substitute in regard to it arises, His sinlessness is emphasized. 2 Corinthians 5:21 tells us that God made Him to be sin for us, but adds that

He *"knew no sin"*. 1 Peter 2:24 tells us that He "His own self bare our sins in His own body on the tree", but assures us that *He "did no sin, neither was guile found in His mouth"* (verse 22). 1 John 3:5 tells us that He was manifested to take away our sins, and adds, *"in Him was no sin."* Surely nothing could be clearer than that no sacrifice but a sinless sacrifice could meet the claims of God's holiness against sin, and if Jesus had not been sinless He could not have stood in the sinner's place; He would not have survived the judgment, and we should have had no Saviour.

The necessity for this sinless offering was foretold in the types and shadows of the Old Testament. The passover lamb had to be without blemish, a male of the first year (Exodus 12:5); and every sacrifice that was offered to God had to be of the same unblemished sort. "If there be any blemish therein, as if it be lame, or blind, or have any ill blemish, thou shalt not sacrifice it unto the Lord thy God" (Deuteronomy 15:21). "But whatsoever hath a blemish, that shall ye not offer: for it shall not be acceptable for you" (Leviticus 22:20). If God could not accept a blemished sacrifice as foreshadowing the sacrifice of Christ, how abhorrent is the thought that He who was the Substance of all the shadows and the Fulfiller of all the types, had a blemish or the taint of sin in Him! And that such a thought might have no place in our minds, we are told that when the time for the offering up of the sacrifice came, He "through the Eternal Spirit offered Himself *without spot* to God" (Hebrews 9:14). Was that offering accepted? It could not have been if it had not been a sinless offering. It was accepted. The Word of God declares that "it is not possible that the blood of bulls and goats should take away sins", but that this Man's one offering hath "perfected for ever them that are sanctified." That one offering was so free from all taint of sin, so essentially, inherently and intrinsically holy and excellent that He having made it has sat down at the right hand of God, never to arise again for such a work; and so complete and efficacious is it, that the Holy Ghost can bear witness that God will remember no more the sins and iniquities of all those that believe, and that through it they have the title now to enter into the very presence of God (Hebrews 10).

## Not Sinless Only but Wholly Good

Now absence of sin would not have been enough, and we cannot stop at the fact that there was no sin, either in the nature or acts of the Man Christ Jesus; we look for positive good, and we are not disappointed. We read, "To him that knoweth to do good and doeth it not, to him it is sin" (James 4:17), and we find this positive goodness in Him at all times and in every circumstance; it was His glory. "He went about doing good, for God was with Him" (Acts 10: 38), and for this He was anointed with the Holy Ghost. He was conceived by and anointed with the Holy Ghost. There is a beautiful type of this in Leviticus 2, where the unleavened cakes mingled with and anointed with oil tell of the life of Jesus, permeated and empowered by the Holy Ghost, of which the oil is a well-known type. The absence of leaven teaches that there was no evil in Him, for leaven is everywhere in Scripture a symbol of evil. Upon these cakes frankincense was put, typical of the fragrance of that goodness that God ever saw in Him. Where every other man *transgressed* and revolted from the known will of God, He could say, "I do always the things that please Him" (John 8:29). Where every other man had *sinned*, and missed God's mark, He could say to His Father, "I have glorified Thee on the earth, I have finished the work which Thou gavest Me to do" (John 17:4); and where every other man had loved *iniquity* and turned out of the right way, it is said of Him, "Thou hast loved righteousness and hated iniquity" (Hebrews 1:9). And there was *no guile* in Him, He was even the same that He said from the beginning (John 8:25).

From the first breath that He drew in the manger until He committed His spirit into His Father's hands at the cross, He was holy unto God. No adverse will within Him ever warred against God's will for Him. No sinful thought or selfish desire ever spoiled the fragrance of His life; there was no fly in that sweet ointment. He was the well-beloved Son in whom was the Father's full delight, doing always the things that pleased Him. He was in the world that reeked with moral putrefaction, surrounded by sin, hated by sinners, assailed by the devil and tested by every trial and He suffered as no other man had suffered or could suffer because of it all;

> *"Yet spotless, undefiled and pure*
> *Our great Redeemer stood;*
> *While Satan's fiery darts He bore,*
> *And did resist to blood."*
> (Isaac Watts, 1674-1748)

The more deeply the life of Jesus is studied, the more impressive does His holy dependence upon God and His obedience to His Word and will appear. And He was obedient without murmuring, though the will of God involved Him in a life of suffering and a death of shame. His heart went out with all that He did. This is beautifully set forth in Isaiah 50, where the Spirit of Christ speaks in the prophet, saying, "The Lord God hath given Me the tongue of the learned, that I should know how to speak a word in season to him that is weary: He wakeneth morning by morning, He wakeneth My ear to hear as the learned. The Lord God hath opened Mine ear, and I was

## THE SINLESSNESS OF THE LORD JESUS: WHY IT MUST BE

not rebellious, neither turned away back. I gave My back to the smiters, and My cheeks to them that plucked off the hair: I hid not My face from shame and spitting" (verses 4-6). In this connection I would quote a beautiful series of the Lord's own sayings that we might contemplate them with wonder and joy.

"My meat and drink is to do the will of Him that sent Me, and to finish His work" (John 4: 34).

"I seek not Mine own will, but the will of the Father which hath sent Me" (5:30).

"I came down from heaven, not to do Mine own will, but the will of Him that sent Me" (6:38).

"The living Father hath sent Me, and I live by the Father" (6:57).

"I and My Father are One" (10:30).

"Father, I thank Thee that Thou hast heard Me. And I knew that Thou hearest Me always" (11:41-42).

"The Father which sent Me, He gave Me a commandment, what I should say, and what I should speak. And I know that His commandment is life everlasting: whatsoever I speak therefore, even as the Father said unto Me, so I speak" (12:49-50).

"That the world may know that I love the Father: and as the Father gave Me commandment, even so I do" (14:31).

"I have kept My Father's commandments, and abide in His love" (15:10).

"I have glorified Thee on the earth; I have finished the work which Thou gavest Me to do" (17: 4).

"It is finished" (19:30).

I might quote many more of these sayings of His, but these are enough to prove to us that He was "the blessed Man" of Psalm 1, that walked not in the counsel of the ungodly, nor stood in the way of sinners, nor sat in the seat of the scornful. But His delight was in the law of the Lord, and in His law did He meditate day and night. In nature and life, in thought and word and deed, in spirit, soul and body He was always and altogether the holy One of God.

Finally think of the testimony that was borne to Him when He was condemned as a malefactor to a cross of shame. Judas the traitor said, "I have betrayed innocent blood" (Matthew 27:4). Pilate the judge said, "Behold, I bring Him forth to you, that ye may know that I find no fault in Him" (John 19:4), and again, "I find no fault in Him" (19:6). And he saith unto them the third time, "Why, what evil hath He done? I find no cause of death in Him" (Luke 23:22). The dying thief said, "This Man hath done nothing amiss" (23:41), and the centurion who carried out the execution exclaimed, "Certainly this was a righteous Man" (23:47), and again, "Truly this was the Son of God" (Matthew 27:54).

# The Temptations of the Lord Jesus

## What Their Character Was

## CONCERNING HIMSELF

The righteous and holy Man, the Son of God, enjoying the privileges proper to such a one, He must undergo the trial of those devices through which the first Adam fell. It is His spiritual condition which is tested. To maintain His position He must have no other will than that of His Father, and fulfil it whatever might be the consequences to Himself. He must fulfil it in the midst of all the difficulties, the privations, the isolation, the desert where Satan's power was, which might tempt Him to follow an easier path than that which should only be for the glory of His Father. He must renounce all the rights that belonged to His own Person, save as He should receive them from God, yielding them up to Him with a perfect trust.—J. N. DARBY [5].

# Chapter 5
# The Temptations of the Lord Jesus

## WHAT THEIR CHARACTER WAS

Some people do not seem able to understand any other sort of temptation than the incitement to do evil, and they argue that temptation can have neither force nor meaning to a man unless there is within him the desire, or at least the liability to yield. We are all familiar with that character of temptation, and it is recognised in the Scriptures, where we read, "Let no man say when he is tempted, I am tempted of God: for God cannot be tempted with evil, neither tempteth He any man: but every man is tempted, when he is drawn away by his own lusts and enticed" (James 1:13-14). Yet we are also told in the same Scriptures, "God did tempt Abraham" when He bade him offer up Isaac (Genesis 22:1). This must have been some other kind of temptation than that of which James speaks; it was certainly not an enticement to do evil; it could not have been, for it is as impossible that God should tempt a man in that way, as it is impossible for Him to lie. It was a testing of what was in Abraham; his faith was put into the crucible and it came out of it, as we know, as gold tried by the fire. And this character of temptation is spoken of more often in the Scriptures than that of enticement to sin.

## The Two Kinds of Temptation

There are two kinds of temptation. Peter speaks of both. He says, "He that hath suffered in the flesh hath ceased from sin" (1 Peter 4:1). That means that when the enticement to sin assails the Christian, instead of gratifying the desire within that answers to the temptation without, he resists it, and suffers in the flesh. He says, "No, Christ suffered for my sins. I will not allow and gratify that which caused Him to suffer the Just for the unjust to bring me to God." But in chapter 1:6-7, he speaks of "manifold temptations"; these are not enticements to do evil, but the trial of the Christian's faith. They are tribulation, distress, persecution, famine, nakedness, perils, sword, pain, bereavement, tears and other burdens and vicissitudes of life (Romans 8:35), by which Christians are tested, and which discover whether God is greater to them than their sorrows and adversities, and nearer to them than their circumstances, and whether they can wholly trust in Him at all times. Plainly, then, temptation is often used in Scripture when enticement to do evil is not the subject at all. Enticement, if yielded to, betrays the bad that is in us, but this other kind of temptation tests us and brings out the good if we really rely upon God, or it may reveal to us our self-confidence and folly, as it did in Peter's case.

Because people do not distinguish between these two kinds of temptation they argue that—since the Scripture says that the Lord Jesus "was in all points tempted like as we are, yet without sin" (Hebrews 2:18; 4:15)—He had to resist the assaults from without, and to watch a traitor within, though He ever fought this two-fold battle successfully. We have heard it said by earnest though unenlightened Christians that in their conflicts with evil they have been comforted by the thought that the Lord had to struggle as they struggle, and that because He overcame in the struggle so may they hope to do. He did indeed overcome in every temptation, but the temptations were entirely from without and never from within as ours so often are; and they certainly may be more than conquerors through Him that loved them, but it will be on other ground entirely from that that they suppose.

### THE LORD TEMPTED APART FROM SIN

This popular teaching is not the truth. It means that there was liability in the Lord to sin even though He did not yield. Such a view of Him is not found in Scripture; it is false; it is derogatory to His holy person and damaging to the faith of His saints. This false idea is chiefly built upon the passage already quoted from Hebrews 4:15; but there is no doubt on the part of those who are able to judge in these matters that the words, "yet without sin", in the Authorised Version, are a faulty translation and should be "sin apart", or "apart from sin". Those who have a Scofield Reference Bible will find it so given in the margin; see also J. N. Darby's New Translation. He was tried by every kind of temptation except that kind. He was never enticed as we are, for there was nothing within Him that answered to sin without, except holy suffering because of it. Our Saviour, High Priest and Leader was and must ever be beyond the possibility of sin. This is the truth that must be emphasised.

The difficulty that some find in understanding any other sort of temptation than enticement to sin may be because they have known no other. Their conflicts have only been with the evil that is within them, the conflict described in Romans 7. They have hardly started on the heavenly pilgrimage, and know little or nothing of the trials of the race of faith: of the discouragements and difficulties of it, and the assaults of Satan in his endeavours to drive those who are in it back from it or turn aside into an easier path. But it is this that is in view in the Hebrew Epistle where we read so much of the way the Lord endured temptation. Christians are not there viewed as struggling in the Slough of Despond, they have got beyond that, and are pilgrims, and warriors, and worshippers; partakers of the heavenly calling, leaving the world behind them and pressing onward to the city that hath foundations, whose builder and maker is God.

Now *Jesus* is the author and finisher of this way of faith. He began at the beginning of it and trod every step of it to its completion, and He knows every trial and difficulty in it, and how Satan besets with many wiles and threatenings those who are following Him in it, for He has experienced them all, and was tempted in all points on that road and in that life of faith, apart from sin, and consequently He is able to sympathise with them and succour them in their hours of weakness and distress and in every time of need.

I quote from *Lectures on Hebrews*, by S. Ridout: "We read of one of Bunyan's characters that at the close of his life said, wherever he had found the footprints of the Lord Jesus, there he had coveted to put his feet. How beautiful that! but sweeter far is the thought that our blessed Lord, when here on earth, searched wherever the feet of His weary saints would have to tread, and He not only coveted to do it, but He did put His feet just there. He has gone through all the circumstances of the wilderness, He knows what all the testing and trials of it mean in a way infinitely beyond the experience of the ripest saint, for He has passed through it, apart from the deadening, dulling, wasteful experiences of sin. We pass through the wilderness, alas, too often yielding to sin. Our blessed Lord passed through, never yielding in thought for one moment to a thing that was not in accordance to His Father's will" [6].

The Lord Jesus led the way in this path of faith and testing and suffering; and this is the meaning of such statements as, "In that He Himself hath suffered being tempted, He is able to succour them that are tempted" (Hebrews 2:18). And again, "Though He were a Son, yet learned He obedience by the things which He suffered" (chapter 5:8). That does not mean that He learnt *to obey*, He never needed lessons of that sort; His very nature was wholly subject to God, but He learnt what obedience entailed in a world that was ruled by the devil, the Prince of the power of the air, the spirit that now worketh in the children of disobedience. He who is the Lord of hosts, came down into a life of obedience and dependence on God, and He was thoroughly tested in it. As every girder in a great bridge is tested before it is put into its destined place in the bridge, so was our Lord tested under the utmost pressure and He was never found wanting. There was no resistance to God's will in Him, no resentment, no murmuring, no fault, no flaw; the will of God did not chafe his Holy soul, He delighted to do it both day and night, and having passed through every test, and graduated in the school of suffering, He has fully qualified to be the author of eternal salvation unto all who obey Him (Hebrews 5:9).

## CONCERNING HIMSELF

### THE TEMPTATION IN THE WILDERNESS

But now leaving that phase of temptation in which we have a part and in which we may have the succour and sympathy of the Lord, we come to the great conflict in the wilderness, when He in whom was all goodness, and who was the God-ordained Leader of the forces of Light met the spirit of evil, the Prince of the powers of darkness. We may learn many lessons as we contemplate these temptations of the Lord; and as we watch His ways we may see how we may overcome, though we must always remember that if we meet Satan at all we meet a defeated foe. Jesus met him when he was flushed with four thousand years of triumph over men. But our subject is not what He was as a pattern for us, but rather what was involved in the conflict for God and men, for Himself and the great adversary.

The Lord had appeared according to the ancient word to "preach the gospel to the poor, to heal the brokenhearted, to preach deliverance to the captives, recovering of sight to the blind, to set at liberty them that are bruised, and to preach the acceptable year of the Lord", but these whom He had come to bless were the devil's captives. He held them as prisoners in his palace, and was "the strong man" who was determined to keep his goods from all molestation. Moreover, he trusted in his armour and thought himself invincible—it is all described by the Lord in a few terse sentences in Luke 11:21-22. For forty centuries he had bound men as captives; he had forged many weapons to effect this and apparently he had done as he wished among them, no one had appeared who could spoil him of his armour or dispute his right to the children of men. The question had been asked by the prophet in former days, "Shall the prey be taken from the mighty? and shall the lawful captives be delivered?" so hopeless did it all

## THE TEMPTATIONS OF THE LORD JESUS:
## WHAT THEIR CHARACTER WAS

seem to be. But Jehovah had answered, "Even the captive of the mighty shall be taken away, and the prey of the terrible shall be delivered ... and all flesh shall know that I the Lord am the Saviour" (Isaiah 49:24-26). But this deliverance of the devil's captives awaited the coming of the One who was "stronger than he", and against whom his most subtlety forged weapons would utterly fail. That Jesus was He, we know, but He had to prove Himself in direct conflict with the devil. Before He could do one public work of mercy or speak one public word of grace this issue had to be tried.

Then further the devil had claimed the kingdoms of the world; he dominated them and arrogated to himself the right to dispose of them as he pleased, but Jesus was the destined and rightful Heir, and the devil knew it; could he out-manœuvre Him and deceive Him and bring Him under his dominion as he had done Adam? He was to be permitted to try, and to tempt the Lord to the utmost of his power, and by his efforts bring into manifestation what was in the heart and mind and will of the Lord, and prove whether He loved righteousness and hated iniquity or not, and whether He was able and worthy to wield the universal sceptre.

And there was still another matter at issue, this second Man had come as the image of the invisible God: as His representative; could He hold the ground for God against all attacks where the first man had basely surrendered his trust? Was God to be glorified in and through man? Would He be able to look upon One, who would sacrifice every worldly advantage, and Himself also, for His will, and overcome the adversary by complete dependence and absolute, unquestioning obedience to the One who had sent Him? This was a great issue, everything in the age-long conflict between good and evil, depended upon it.

In this encounter with Satan, Jesus was alone and wholly dependent upon God; no disciple was near to cheer Him and no angel ministered to Him until the fight was finished. This isolation from all aid from others is emphasised by the fact that He was carried into the wilderness by the Spirit to meet the foe: away from the abodes of men to the haunts of the wild beasts. And the fact that the temptation is recorded in the Synoptic Gospels and not in that of John, would teach us that it was in His manhood-weakness and dependence upon God that the fight was waged, and not by the Godhead power that dwelt in Him; for John's Gospel is the Gospel of His divine glory, the glory of the Son brought down into Manhood; while the Synoptic Gospels show us the same Person, truly, but as "the woman's Seed", the lowly Man of sorrows, who had no resources but in God.

### The First Temptation

It has often been said that in these three temptations of the Lord "all that is in the world: 1, the lust of the flesh; 2, the lust of the eyes; 3, the pride of life" appear; and I have no doubt that this is true, for these three phases of the world are the weapons in which the devil trusts in his enslavement of men, and it is in this order that they are recorded in Luke's Gospel, which gives us the moral and not the historical order of them.

In the proposal that Jesus should make the stones into bread there was a subtle suggestion of kindly interest in His welfare as well as a reflection upon God, as there had been when he tempted Eve in Eden. Are you the Son of God and hungry? Surely God has forgotten you, or is indifferent to your need! Use the power you possess and relieve your hunger. Thus might the temptation be paraphrased. It was met by a perfect answer, "It is written that man shall not live by bread alone, but by every word of GOD" (Luke 4:4). God and His word were all to Jesus, He would not use His power on His own behalf or to take Himself out of the place of dependence upon God. He could endure hunger but not independence of God. He sought no ease or comfort for Himself, His meat and drink were the will of God and to finish His work. The lust of the flesh had no place in His heart nor was there a joint in His armour where a doubt as to God's goodness could be thrust; and where Adam and Eve were overthrown and wounded to death, Jesus stood firm and unscathed.

## THE SECOND TEMPTATION

In the second temptation the world's kingdoms were set before His eyes, with all the power and pomp and splendour of them, which dazzle and fascinate men, and for which they will sell their souls and deny their God. And these kingdoms all belonged to Jesus, but God's way, and the only way by which He could secure them in everlasting righteousness was by suffering and death. "You shall have them", said the tempter, "by an easy way. I will give them to you if you will but worship me; acknowledge me as greater than yourself and God; take them from my hand and all shall be yours." But those glittering kingdoms had no attraction in that hour for the holy One of God. He would not take them from any hand but God's hand, He could trust God to put all things beneath His feet when the due time came, but that time was not yet. His eyes were upon God, and He met the temptation with an uncompromising answer, "It is written, Thou shalt worship the Lord thy God and Him only shalt thou serve" (Luke 4:8).

## The Third Temptation

The third temptation was the most subtle of the three, and the devil backed it up by a partly quoted text. He proposed that the Lord should cast Himself down from a pinnacle of the temple, and by such an exploit gain a double advantage—put God to the test, and prove Him, as to whether You are the special object of His care according to the word quoted, and at the same time convince the multitude in the courtyard of the temple that You are the Messiah, the Son of God. The trap was laid in vain, and His answer, "It is written, thou shalt not tempt the Lord thy God" (Luke 4:12; Matthew 4:7), showed how thoroughly Jesus perceived the devil's purpose. It was no business of His to put God's word to the test to see whether God would honour it or not, no doubt as to it ever entered His mind, it did not need to be proved to Him; nor was it His business to vindicate Himself before the people. "My times are in Thy hands" was the whole spirit of His life and activities, and He would not take them out of God's hands.

GOD was the answer of this ever dependent and so ever victorious Man. He looked to GOD for His sustenance; GOD filled His heart to the exclusion of all other glory; His whole confidence and trust was in GOD; God's will was His law, God's way was His delight; He set the Lord always before Him and He was not moved. It was thus that He was tested and came through the testing stronger than the foe. By resisting all the efforts of "the strong man" to turn Him from His devotion to God, He bound him fast and went forth in the power of the Spirit to make his goods His spoil; for the grace and mercy of God showed themselves in Him and He went about doing good and delivering all that were oppressed of the devil.

## THE TEMPTATIONS OF THE LORD JESUS:
## WHAT THEIR CHARACTER WAS

He was in the midst of men as a living Deliverer, the Master of Satan who had oppressed them so long.

How miserable and inadequate and dishonouring to the Lord is the teaching that He met no personal devil in the wilderness, but merely retired into it to consider various schemes by which He might press His claims upon men and prove His Messiahship to them, and that the temptations were nothing more than plans of campaign that He considered and rejected.

### THE FINAL TEMPTATION

But the overcoming in the wilderness was not the end of the conflict, the devil wielded the power of death and by it kept men in bondage all their life-time for fear of it. And Jesus had come to wrench that power from him, and He could only do this by dying. It was not a living Deliverer that could emancipate men from the tyrant's power—blinded by the devil they rejected Him in that character—but a dying Redeemer. He had come to die, this only was the way of obedience to God and of love to men. And it was as the shadow of that death crept darkly over His path that Satan returned to the attack, to tempt Him to draw back from that way of suffering. The horror and shame and woe unspeakable that lay before Him pressed heavily upon the spirit of the Lord, and He began to show to His disciples that it was to a cross and not to a throne that He was progressing. And Satan seized the occasion, and using the impetuous and unwary Peter as his spokesman he endeavoured to turn the Lord from His fixed purpose to do the will of God even to death. "This be far from Thee (pity Thyself), this shall not be unto Thee." But the Lord detected the foe in that friendly guise, and the temptation to think of Himself was met with stern rebuke, "Get thee behind Me, Satan", and then to Peter, "thou savourest not the things that be of God" (Matthew 16:22-23). As in the wilderness before He entered upon His public service so now at the end of it, God was the sole object of His life.

It was in this same spirit of dependence and full subjection to the will of God that He went through the agony of Gethsemane, when Satan marshalled all the powers of darkness to appal Him and drive Him back from making the great sacrifice; but He came out of the trial saying, "The cup which My Father hath given Me shall I not drink it?" (John 18:11). And so onward to the cross. In the days of His flesh He "offered up prayers and supplications with a strong crying and tears unto Him who was able to save Him *out of death*, and was heard in that He feared" for His piety—His whole-hearted dependence upon God and His trust in Him (Hebrews 5:7). Satan was utterly foiled, he was beaten at every point in the field, and Jesus, whom he could neither decoy nor drive from the path of God's will, through death has destroyed him that had the power of death, that He might deliver them who through the fear of death were all their life-time subject to bondage, and become the author of eternal salvation to all who obey Him. He went down into death, committing Himself into His Father's hands, and the Father's glory has raised Him from the dead, and now He can say to all who bow down before Him, "Fear not; I am the first and the last: I am He that liveth and was dead, and, behold, I am alive for evermore, Amen; and have the keys of hell and of death" (Revelation 1:17-18).

And the devil is a defeated foe. He has no authority or power over the saints; he

> *"trembles when he sees*
> *The weakest saint upon his knees."*
> *(William Cowper, 1731-1800)*

## THE TEMPTATIONS OF THE LORD JESUS: WHAT THEIR CHARACTER WAS

They have but to resist him and he will flee from them, for they are no longer his prey, but the blood-purchased possession of the Saviour who has delivered them, and they are to share in all the results of the great victory of the Lord over him for "The God of peace shall shortly bruise Satan under their feet" (Romans 16:20).

## CONCERNING HIMSELF

# The Miracles of the Lord Jesus
## What They Prove

Each discourse, each miracle, nay each word and act, is a fresh ray of glory streaming forth from the Person of the Word through the veil of His flesh. The Incarnation is the one great wonder; other miracles follow as a matter of course. The real marvel would be if the Incarnate Being should work no miracles; as it is they are the natural results of His presence among men, rather than its higher manifestation.—H. P. LIDDON [7].

# Chapter 6
# The Miracles of the Lord Jesus
## WHAT THEY PROVE

A miracle is an act of superhuman power. All the miracles of the Lord Jesus were such, and were the attestation of His person and mission. He had come forth from the Father, and come into the world, and His miracles were the proof of this. They were His Father's works, as His arresting and challenging words to the Jews declared, "If I do not the works of My Father, believe Me not. But if I do, though ye believe not Me, believe the works; that ye may know and believe that the Father is in Me, and I in Him" (John 10:37-38). The Holy Ghost speaking through Simon Peter on the day of Pentecost described these works as "miracles, wonders and signs which God did by Him". They were works of power that amazed the people, and were signs to them that God had come down to them in mercy.

Modernists refuse to accept the miraculous. They hold that there are "laws of nature" that are immutable and cannot be overruled or suspended, and that what appeared to be miracles in former days were simply the operations of certain of these laws which were unknown to the majority of people at the time. They would instance the fact that the solemn tramp of the soldiers' feet at the funeral of King George was heard in the uttermost ends of the earth as plainly as in the streets of London. One hundred years ago such an idea would have been laughed at as the conception of a madman. Yes, but the works of the Lord were not on such a plane as that; they were wrought in another realm; they were addressed to the needs and miseries of men, which were the result of sin having entered into the world. They were not a challenge to immutable laws but the revelation of infinite mercy in the One to whom all the prophets bore witness. When doubts assailed the imprisoned Baptist and he sent his disciples to Jesus, saying, Art Thou He that should come, or look we for another? He answered, "Go your way, and tell John what things ye have seen and heard, how that the blind see, the lame walk, the lepers are cleansed, the deaf hear, the dead are raised, to the poor the Gospel is preached. And blessed is he, whosoever shall not be offended in Me" (Luke 7:19-23).

He who did these things was the One who had created all things, "For by Him were all things created, that are in heaven and that are in earth, visible and invisible ... all things were created by Him and for Him ... and by Him all things consist" (Colossians 1:16-17), and amongst the "all things" were these laws of nature that bind the universe together for its good. They are His laws and must surely be subservient to Him, for He who made them controls them, they all subsist in Him. In them is declared the wisdom of the Creator. They have been there from the beginning of creation for men to discover and make use of, and, when discovered, they ought to have had the effect of turning men into worshippers of the One who created them, and making them ashamed of themselves that they had not discovered them before. Instead of which, men are puffed up with pride as though they had invented them themselves. And yet what an immeasurable gulf the ability to discover and make use of these laws puts between man and the beasts.

Whatever laws there may be in the physical universe, one thing is certain, the law of man's relation to his Creator and God was disturbed by his disobedience in Eden. Then there entered into his being and his relations with God and with his fellows and with nature what had not been there before. "By one man sin entered into the world and death by sin; and death passed upon all men, for that all have sinned" (Romans 5:12). "The law of sin and death" (Romans 8:2) began then to exercise its inexorable power in the lives of men; they were affected by it spiritually, morally and physically. Tears, death, sorrow, crying and pain (Revelation 21:4), as well as enmity against God, and the curse which fell upon the whole earth, were the result of this invasion of man's life by sin; these things affect him in this life, and "after this the judgment" (Hebrews 9:27). It was to this state of things that the Lord addressed Himself when He came into the world. The object of His coming was to deliver men from all oppression; to reveal what God is in His very nature; to restore the broken relationship with God, and to bring men back into full suitability to God, as the Scriptures declare, "God was in Christ, reconciling the world to Himself, not imputing their trespasses unto them" (2 Corinthians 5:19). If miracles were a means to this end, which was God's great purpose, what power could prevent them? This reconciling men to God was the greatest of all miracles.

It is against the intervention of God for the blessing of men that modernism opposes its subtle forces. And with this in view it must explain away the miracles. I give an instance of this. In a paper entitled "The Spirit of God and the Healing of Disease" appearing, regrettably enough, in an evangelical magazine, we are treated to the following:—

> "It is recorded by St. Luke in Chapter 13. A woman came to the synagogue suffering from an infirmity or weakness. The complaint was of long standing—eighteen years. Jesus described her as a daughter of Abraham whom Satan had bound. With our present knowledge we should say, 'In the grip of a false idea, making weakness instead of health God's will for her.' The cure was not easy even for Jesus. When He saw her, He called her and said, 'Woman, thou art loosed from thine infirmity.' But she was not cured. Then Jesus evidently came down from the platform into the body of the synagogue where the woman was, and laid His hand upon her. In this way His vision of perfect health inspired her. His mighty faith overcame her timidity and she was healed."

Passing over the obvious distortion of the Divinely-given record, which says nothing about the cure not being easy, nor the woman not being cured at the word of the Lord, nor His having to step down from the platform to accomplish it—to that which is worse, we must conclude, if we accept this author's view, that we, *with our present knowledge,* know more than the Lord did about infirmity and disease, and that what He accomplished in the healing of the woman He did as a clever psychologist or Christian Scientist and not as the Sovereign Lord, "the Son of God, manifested that He might destroy the works of the devil" (1 John 3:8).

## THE MIRACLES OF THE LORD JESUS: WHAT THEY PROVE

It is all of one piece with the general attack upon the glory and the person of our Lord, His infallibility and omniscience, and upon the character of His mission to men. It is worse than that. If the Lord wrought His miracles by suggestion, and by using powers that are available to any who care to exercise them and not by Divine power, He must have known this, and consequently He was a deceiver when He said, "the works that I do in My Father's Name, they bear witness of Me" (John 10:25). "The Father that dwelleth in Me, He doeth the works ... believe Me for the very works' sake" (14:10-11).

All the Lord's miracles were works of mercy, with the exception of the cursing of the fig tree (Mark 11:12-20), and some great significance lay behind that act. It was with the fig leaves that Adam and Eve endeavoured to clothe their nakedness after their disobedience and fall in Eden, and the Jews' religion had degenerated into the effort to secure by ritual and works of the law a covering for their moral and spiritual nakedness, while remaining alienated from God and disobedient to Him. That whole system of the Jews' religion that had no room for Christ and refused to yield to Him the glory that was His due, was condemned by God, as are all the efforts of men to cover their sin and obtain righteousness by works. We, who believe the Scriptures, know that the only covering for sin and the souls of sinners is atonement by blood. The word translated atonement in the Scriptures means, a covering. I suggest that the cursing of the fig tree was a symbolical act, teaching us these great and fundamental facts. The time and circumstances in which it was done seem to confirm this.

The beginning of His miracles was in Cana of Galilee (John 2:1-11), and by it He manifested His glory—"The people which sat in darkness saw a great light, and to them which sat in the region and shadow of death, light sprang up" (Matthew 4:16)—and His disciples believed on Him. It was a remarkable miracle, this turning the water into wine at the marriage feast. He had ordained the marriage tie at the beginning, and though it had become sadly marred by sin, He hallowed it by His presence. They were not great or rich, this couple who called Jesus to their marriage; indeed the fact that they had no wine would indicate that they were very poor; but Jesus was the Friend of the poor, as He is to this day, and He manifested His glory by caring for them in their need and raising the joy of their marriage day to a level they could not have known if He had not been there. "He provided a fit accompaniment, provided it of the best, and in such large measure as has alarmed and amazed the moralist. The quality and the greatness of the gift were worthy of God; and we see the generosity all the more clearly when we remember that this bountiful Creator had a little while before refused to create bread to relieve Himself of hunger" (Nicholl [8]).

The glory that began to shine at Cana shed a greater brightness at the close of those eventful years, when His foes pressed about Him to arrest Him. Malchus, the servant of the high priest, would hold a commission from his master to go with Judas into the garden and lead the multitude that went out to capture the Lord. How astonished Peter must have been when he saw Judas step out of the crowd and put the traitor-kiss upon his Lord. He did not know how to deal with Judas, but he had no hesitation as to how to treat Malchus, when he, vaunting his temporary authority, laid hands upon the Lord, and in the name of the high priest directed the band to make Him prisoner. At such audacity Peter's indignation flamed hotly, and drawing his sword, he aimed one mighty blow at the dastard, meaning to lay him dead at his feet, cleft through the skull.

It was new work for the fisherman, he had not been trained to wield a sword, and his misdirected energy only resulted in the loss of an ear to Malchus, and the exposure of his own impetuous folly, and, shall we add, his true love for his Master. But there was yet another result. The Lord had said, "I must work the works of Him that sent Me while it is day: the night cometh when no man can work. As long as I am in the world I am the light of the world" (John 9:4-5). The gloom of night was gathering thickly upon the world, but He was still its light, and there was one more work of mercy that He must do before the devil and men had their way, a work not to be wrought upon a friend but upon a foe, who had come against Him with murder in his heart. Hence, with a word of gentle rebuke to Peter, He stretched forth His hand and touched the severed ear and healed it (John 18:10-11; Luke 22:50-51). Here was the miracle of all miracles, of good triumphing over evil, of Divine and infinite mercy pouring out itself upon men in the very height and venom of their sin.

"Wist ye not that I must be about My Father's business" (Luke 2:49) are the first words that are recorded as having come from His mouth in the Gospel of Luke, in which Gospel alone is the *healing* of the ear recorded. That business was blessing and not judgment; it was healing and not a sword. The audacity of Malchus and the impetuosity of Peter only served as an opportunity for the continued goodness that was in Him, and, having done that work, He submitted Himself to His foes, and they bound with cords His hands that had only been stretched out to bless, and led Him away to mockery and shame and crucifixion.

The works of the Lord were such as no other man did (John 15:24) and they left those who saw them without excuse. What wonderful works they were! but the way in which they were done was even more wonderful than the works. And how the hearts of those who were the subjects of them must have been moved by them, unless they remained dead in spite of them. Consider what the feelings of the leper must have been when the Lord, moved with compassion, stretched forth His hand and laid it upon him saying, "I will, be thou clean" (Mark 1:41). Could any other man have done that? If the leper had come near to Peter, he would have cried, "Keep away from me." If he had approached to John, he would have said, "Away, don't come near to me." The leper's touch would have contaminated any other man, but the hand and word of Jesus drove the foul disease away. What must have been the feelings of Jairus and his wife when the Lord took their dead daughter by the hand and said, "Maid, arise", and showed, not His power only, but His consideration for the child when He commanded them to give her meat (Luke 8:54-55). Think of His care for the people who were faint by the way, when He provided them with such a meal as they had never had before, and that out of five loaves and two small fishes. Yet, though He created by His divine power, He would permit no waste. The fragments left over from that meal must be gathered up for another (John 6:12-13).

Stand by and behold Him when He said to the widowed woman, bereaved of her only son, "Weep not", and then, turning to the dead son, said, "Young man, I say unto thee, arise." He might have claimed the life and service of the young man, and added, "Follow Me", but He did not, He delivered him to his mother (Luke 7:13-15). What heart could have remained unmoved that saw His cheeks wet with tears as Mary of Bethany bowed down in her sorrow at His feet; or remained unthrilled with a hitherto unfelt triumph when He cried with a loud voice, "Lazarus, come forth." We can easily conceive the astonishment and excitement of the crowd when the dead man answered that loud command and came forth from his tomb; but Jesus was not excited. His quiet word to those that stood by to loose him from the grave clothes and let him go, showed how calm He was, and how considerate for Lazarus in his strange circumstances (John 11:32-44). It is not easy to say whether the compassion of His heart or the power of His word, or His gentle consideration for His friend would command the greatest admiration on that great occasion.

While the people confessed, "He hath done all things well" (Mark 7:37), the motive behind the works they did not understand. Even His brethren misjudged Him: they said to Him, "There is no man that doeth anything in secret, and he himself seeketh to be known openly. If Thou do these things, show Thyself to the world" (John 7:4). They could not understand One who sought not His own glory (8:50) and would not have the honour that comes from men (5:41), and who did the works only that they might believe that the Father had sent Him (5:36), for beyond the deliverance from their physical sufferings was the need of souls of the knowledge of God. Yet His glory could not be hid, it shone in the works that He did, for if they were the Father's works, who could do these but the Son? His works bore witness to the fact that the Father had sent the Son to be the Saviour of the world (1 John 4:14). And because the world was such as it was, only the Father's sent One could be its Saviour, and having come, He must of necessity work miracles in it, for God is love.

We might rightly have challenged His claim to have come from the Father if He had moved with apparent indifference amid the miseries of men, if He had left the leper to his corruption, the blind to his darkness, and the cripple to his weakness; if He had not been moved to compassion by the widow's tears, if He had not wept with Mary, and smiled upon the children. But His words, "My Father worketh hitherto and I work" (John 5:17) reveal the indissoluble oneness that existed in all things between the Father and the Son; and these works of mercy for the blessing of men were among these all things. They were the Father's works.

His miracles all declared what the feelings of God were towards His creatures in their miseries, and though they were wrought in vain as far as the nation in which they were done was concerned, they abide for us in the record of them in the Holy Scriptures; that we may read of them and meditate upon them and rejoice in that great salvation, "which first began to be spoken by the Lord, and was confirmed unto us by them that heard Him; God also bearing them witness both by signs and wonders and divers miracles, and gifts of the Holy Ghost according to His own will" (Hebrews 2:3-4).

# The Deity of the Lord Jesus
## In the Gospel of John

## CONCERNING HIMSELF

In the four Gospels, says St. Augustine, or rather in the four books of the one Gospel, the Apostle John, deservedly compared to an eagle by reason of his spiritual understanding, has lifted the enunciation of truth to a far higher and sublimer point than the other three, and by this elevation he would fain have our hearts lifted up likewise. For the other three Evangelists walked, so to speak, on earth with our Lord as Man. Of His Godhead they said but few things. But John, as if he found it oppressive to walk on earth, has opened his treatise as it were with a peal of thunder; he has raised himself not merely above the earth, and the whole compass of the air and heaven, but even above the angel-host, and every order of the invisible powers, and has reached even to Him by whom all things were made, in that sentence, "In the beginning was the Word."— H. P. LIDDON [7].

## Chapter 7
## The Deity of the Lord Jesus
### IN THE GOSPEL OF JOHN

In the history of the Church on earth no greater theologian than Athanasius ever arose to champion the truth of God against error, yet great and faithful as he was, he confessed that "whenever he forced his understanding to meditate on the Divinity (Deity) of the Logos (the Word) his toilsome and unavailing efforts recoiled on themselves; that the more he thought the less he comprehended; and the more he wrote, the less capable was he of expressing his thoughts" (Gibbon [9]). We do not wonder at that when we consider the immeasurable greatness of the Subject and the limited capacity of man's understanding.

This inability of the human mind by its own effort to discover and know God was clearly recognised by men of intelligence in ancient times. Zophar the Naamathite challenged Job as to it, when he asked, "Canst thou by searching find out God? Canst thou find out the Almighty to perfection?" (Job 11:7). And Agur the son of Jakeh appealed to Ithiel (whose name meant, There is a God) for help when he confessed his ignorance of God. "I have neither learned wisdom," said he, "nor have I the knowledge of the Holy. Who hath ascended up into heaven and descended? Who hath gathered the wind in His fists; who hath bound the waters in a garment? Who hath established the ends of the earth? What is His name and what is His Son's Name, if thou canst tell?" (Proverbs 30:3-4). As far as we know Ithiel had no answer to that appeal.

The modern mind is not more capable in itself of grasping the *things of God* than were these great men of old, for "It is written, Eye hath not seen, nor ear heard, neither hath entered into the heart of man, the things which God hath prepared for them that love Him" (1 Corinthians 2:9). And if the things of God are outside man's range, how infinitely above him must God Himself—the Father and His Son—be! And yet we must know Him; the awakened soul is conscious that all its blessing lies in the knowledge of God, and pants for this knowledge as the hart pants for the water brooks (Psalm 42:1).

When "the Word became flesh" and dwelt among men (John 1:14), He revealed the great secret as to how God was to be known when He said, "I thank Thee, O Father, Lord of heaven and earth, because Thou hast hid these things from the wise and prudent and hast revealed them unto babes. Even so, Father, for so it seemed good in Thy sight" (Matthew 11:25-26). These words from the lips of the Lord Himself declare that the knowledge of God cannot be gained by laborious and brain-wearying investigation, no matter how sincere the labour may be, but only by revelation; they strike at the root of the pride of the human intellect and prick the bubble of those who, "vainly puffed up in their fleshly minds", reject the revelation and think to find out God by their own searching; they shut out the reasonings and imaginations of the self-confident mind, which always, alas, since man is fallen, and "alienated in his mind by wicked works", exalts itself against the true knowledge of God (Colossians 2:18; 1:21; 2 Corinthians 10:5). They show that there are two sides to the fact of revelation. There is activity on God's part and receptivity on ours. God is revealed and the babes receive the revelation. The light shines and there are eyes that admit it. The truth is declared, but it is also believed. God must speak and men must hear, for "faith cometh by hearing and hearing by the word of God" (Romans 10:17). And we are as dependent upon God for the babe-nature and the opened eyes and the believing heart, and the listening ears, as we are for the revelation that these perceive, appreciate and appropriate.

In Old Testament times there were certain limited revelations of God's attributes and ways. The heavens declared the glory of His power, and firmament showed His handiwork (Psalm 19:1). The law given at Sinai announced the uprightness of His kingdom and the justice of His throne. He showed Himself often in His providential care for men and as the covenant-keeping God; and proclaimed His Name, "The Lord, the Lord God, merciful and gracious, longsuffering, and abundant in goodness and truth" (Exodus 34:6). But these partial revelations, rays from the eternal splendour, only served to make those who received them cry out for a fuller, a complete knowledge of His heart and nature, as when Moses said, "Show me Thy glory" (Exodus 33:18), and David pleaded, "O send out Thy light and Thy truth; let them lead me, let them bring me unto Thy holy hill and to Thy tabernacles" (Psalm 43:3). Those soul longings have been answered in a manner that neither Moses nor David could have conceived. The glory has appeared and the light and the truth have come in the Son of God, for "God who at sundry times and in divers manners spake in times past unto the fathers by the prophets hath in these last times spoken unto us by His Son ... Who being *the brightness of His glory*, and the express image of His person" (Hebrews 1:1-3). "No man hath seen God at any time; the only-begotten Son which is in the bosom of the Father, He hath declared Him" (John 1:18). And the Son in whom God has spoken and who has declared what God is in His very nature and has glorified Him on the earth, said, *"I am the light of the world"* (8:12), and *"I am the truth"* (14:6).

We are dependent upon the Holy Scripture for all our knowledge of this full revelation, for we were not on earth when the Son of God dwelt among men, but the Father sent forth the Holy Spirit to inspire and guide the men who companied with Him to bear an infallible witness to what they heard and saw. "That which we have heard," wrote one of them, "Which we have seen with our eyes, which we have looked upon, and our hands have handled of the Word of life ... declare we unto you" (1 John 1:1-3).

There is a peculiar dignity and authority about the Scriptures. It could not be otherwise, since they are the words of the living and almighty God. For instance, they do not set out to prove that God is, they state the fact and show the effect of His presence and power, and they tell us that it is only the fool—the man void of all understanding—that says in his heart, "There is no God" (Psalm 14:1). They open with that majestic statement, "In the beginning God created the heavens and the earth." The New Testament is more than the equal of the Old, in this dignity and authority. It does not set out to prove that the One we know as Jesus is God, equally with the Father and the Holy Ghost, it states the fact and shows the effect of it. So that the Gospel which I think may be justly called the greatest book in the New Testament, opens with the sublime statement, "In the beginning was the Word; and the Word was with God; and the Word was God."

The "beginning" of Genesis signifies the moment when the voice of God called the worlds into being, and the pendulum of Time began to swing, but the opening words of John's Gospel carries us further back than that and tell us that when the first creatorial word was uttered the Word was there. Whatever may have been the activities of the Godhead anterior to creation, He had His part in them, for then He was with God, His delight and companion (Proverbs 8:22-31), and He was God, His equal, "His Fellow" (Zechariah 13:7), in all things purposed and done—in His existence He is eternal, in His nature He is divine; in His person, He is distinct. "All things were made by Him." His was the voice that commanded and it was done. That creative life-giving energy which abides only in God, wrought with divine power and wisdom through Him; "and without Him was not anything made that was made" (John 1:3).

Two other passages in the New Testament definitely and fully predicate the creation of all things to Him. In one of them, words are taken up from the Old Testament (Psalm 102:25-27), "And Thou, Lord, in the beginning hast laid the foundations of the earth, and the heavens are the works of Thy hand: they shall perish; but Thou remainest; and they all shall wax old as a garment; and as a vesture shalt Thou fold them up, and they shall be changed: but Thou art the same, and Thy years fail not" (Hebrews 1:10-12). This ascription to Him, who creates for His own purpose and dissolves what He has created when it has served that purpose, but who abides, unchanging and eternal in His person and being, occurs in an Epistle addressed to Hebrew Christians, that they might be properly impressed with the glory of their Lord and the greatness of the salvation that they had in Him. The other passage was written to Gentile believers and tells us "By Him were all things created that are in heaven and that are in earth, visible and invisible, whether they be thrones, or dominions, or principalities, or powers, all things were created by Him, and for Him; and He is before all things, and by Him all things consist" (Colossians 1:16-17). Jew and Gentile alike must recognise and acknowledge His glory, and none who believe, whether Jew or Gentile, must have any doubt as to the greatness of the One whom they have confessed as Lord and Saviour. He is God the Creator: as to power, almighty; as to wisdom, infinite; as to authority, supreme; as to being, eternal.

The opening of John's Gospel could not be plainer in its statements than it is, and they are framed by the wisdom of the Holy Spirit to meet every opposition to the truth that might arise in the human heart. Interest is awakened by these statements as to whether any on earth would believe and confess the truth of them as they were known and confessed in heaven, and we may be sure that heaven was engrossed in this same question. As we pass from page to page of the Gospel, we see a ray of the light break first into one heart and then into another; here a man and there a woman is brought to bow in worship at the feet of the Sovereign Lord of all, and so to confess that He is indeed God; but it is not until the end of the Gospel is reached (chapter 21 is a beautiful postscript to it), that His disciples behold Him and own Him in His full glory. On that second "first day of the week" the disciples were gathered together, and Thomas the unbeliever with them. In disposition and temper he was a veritable materialist and had declared that he would believe nothing that he could not see and handle. Then Jesus stood in the midst, and showed to the astonished eyes of his obstinate follower the wounds that He had sustained in His death and which remained in His incorruptible body. It was enough for Thomas; he was an infidel no longer, but falling down before his Master, he voiced the faith and adoration of all his brethren in those true and memorable words, "My Lord and My God."

If the Lord Jesus had not been what Thomas confessed Him to be, but only a good and true man, He would have rebuked him for uttering foolish words, for it would have been an unspeakable wickedness for one man to accept from another man that adoration which only belongs to God; but He did accept it, because it was His right, and He went further and declared the blessedness of all those throughout the ages who should perceive His glory and confess it and render like homage to Him: saying, "Thomas, because thou hast seen Me, thou hast believed: blessed are they that have not seen, yet have believed." In this great and convincing incident we see how the end of the Gospel answers to the opening word of it.

The place that the Lord Jesus, the Son of the Father, has in the thoughts and affections of the Father and the Holy Ghost is instructive. I will quote certain passages from the Gospel of John which show that He was the worthy and adequate Object of the Father's love when on earth and the One for whose glory the Holy Ghost labours now. "We beheld His glory, the glory as of the only-begotten of the Father" (1:14); "The only-begotten Son which is in the bosom of the Father" (1:18); "The Father loveth the Son, and hath given all things into His hands" (3:35); "The Father loveth the Son, and showeth Him all things that Himself doeth" (5:20); "The living Father hath sent

Me, and I live by the Father" (6:57); "The Father hath not left Me alone" (8:29); "Therefore doth My Father love Me because I lay down My life" (10:17); "I and My Father are One" (10:30). And that we might know that this love that the Father had for Him and the delight that He had in Him were not confined to His life on earth, He said, "Father ... Thou lovedst Me before the foundation of the world" (17:24).

But now that He has gone back to the Father we learn that the Holy Ghost has come from thence to bear witness to Him. As the Father once looked down upon Him, so now the Holy Ghost looks up to Him, and would turn the eyes of all His disciples in the same direction. We read, "But the Comforter, which is the Holy Ghost, whom the Father will send in My Name, He shall teach you all things, and bring all things to your remembrance, *whatsoever I have said unto you*" (14:26). "But when the Comforter is come, whom I will send unto you from the Father, even the Spirit of truth which proceedeth from the Father, *He shall testify of Me*" (15:26). "Howbeit when He, the Spirit of truth, is come, He will guide you into all truth: for He shall not speak of Himself; but whatsoever He shall hear, that shall He speak: and He will show you things to come. *He shall glorify Me: for He shall receive of Mine, and shall show it unto you. All things that the Father hath are Mine: therefore said I, that He shall take of Mine, and shall show it unto you*" (16:13-15).

The revelation of God is complete, and we know God now as Father, Son and Holy Ghost: three Persons yet one God. It was this that came into full manifestation when Jesus was here, for "in Him all the fulness (of the Godhead) was pleased to dwell" (Colossians 1:19, see also Colossians 2:10, N.Tr.), and "God was manifest in the flesh" (1 Timothy 3:16).

### THE DEITY OF THE LORD JESUS: IN THE GOSPEL OF JOHN

The Father is the source of all blessing *for* men.

The Son has brought the blessing *to* men.

The Holy Ghost makes the blessing good *in* men.

Each Person in the Godhead is engaged in making the revelation a reality in the souls of men, for we read, "No man knoweth the Father save THE SON and he to whomsoever the Son will reveal Him" (Matthew 11:27). "Blessed art thou, Simon Barjona: for flesh and blood hath not revealed this unto thee, but MY FATHER which is in heaven" (Matthew 16:17). "God hath revealed them unto us by HIS SPIRIT: for the Spirit searcheth all things, yea, the deep things of God" (1 Corinthians 2:10).

The Holy Spirit dwells within the believer, a power commensurate with the love that moved the Father to send the Son, and works in the hearts of those who have humbly yielded to the Lord, so that they are not now groping in darkness, or wearying themselves in a vain search after God by human effort, for the true light is shining and "the love of God is shed abroad in our hearts by the Holy Ghost" (Romans 5:5). "And we know that the Son of God is come, and hath given us an understanding, that we should know Him that is true; and we are in Him that is true, even in His Son Jesus Christ. *This is the true God and eternal life.* Children, keep yourselves from idols" (1 John 5:20-21).

## CONCERNING HIMSELF

# The Death of the Lord Jesus
## Atonement by Blood

It has been truly said, there is nothing like the cross. It stands and shall stand for ever in all its solitary greatness and grandeur, the wonder of every intelligent creature, and the pillar upon which is indelibly inscribed the evil and hatred of fallen man and the goodness and love of God. There appears the greatest sin that man ever committed and there is the mightiest display of mercy on the part of God that ever came to light. It is the place where man was tested in every spring of his moral being, and it is where the compassions of God were sounded to their depths. There man lifted up impious hand and struck at his Creator with deadly intent, and the answer of God was given in unspeakable, infinite and victorious love.—J. BOYD [10].

> *"The very spear that pierced His side*
> *Drew forth the blood to save."*
> *(James George Deck, 1802-1884)*

# Chapter 8
# The Death of the Lord Jesus

## ATONEMENT BY BLOOD

*"And behold a throne was set in heaven, and one sat on the throne, and He that sat was to look upon like a jasper and a sardine stone"* (Revelation 4:2-3). It is my conviction that if the glorious and eternally blessed Occupant of that throne had appeared only as the jasper stone—the clear, unsullied crystal—no created being could have stood before Him, but because the blood-red rays of the sardine blend with the light of the jasper, the worst of sinners may have a footing there in everlasting righteousness and peace. To understand what the symbol illustrates take the great Christian message which is declared to us in 1 John 1:5, "God is light and in Him is no darkness at all." There is the clear shining of the crystal, but if that had been all could any man have abode in the searching brightness of it? But there follows at once the fear-dispelling, peace-giving word, "The blood of Jesus Christ, His Son, cleanseth us from all sin." How perfectly that great fact harmonises and blends with the light! Indeed it is part of it. What confidence it gives to the soul, and what uprightness! For in the light nothing can be hidden, yet

all is covered by the blood, it is the perfect atonement, equal in its efficacy to the full shining of the light. In the knowledge of this the one who believes walks in the light even as God is in the light and can rejoice in the supremacy of the throne that shines as the jasper and the sardine stone.

Had sin never entered into the world there would, of course, have been no need for atonement by blood, and according to our estimate of what sin is will be our appreciation of it. If a man thinks that sin is merely "the survival of the tiger in humanity" which evolution will most surely destroy, as some divinity professors have asserted, he will deny all need of it; if he thinks that a man's sin is nothing more than weakness, or a mere negation that he may overcome in time, he will resent the word that tells him that he needs a Saviour such as Jesus is; but if he discovers that his deeds are the outward evidence of a corrupted inward nature, and that his "sin is lawlessness" as the Bible says it is, "for every one that doeth sin doeth lawlessness" (1 John 3:4, RV); if his soul bows down before the truth that "by one man sin entered into the world and death by sin, and death passed upon all men for that all have sinned" (Romans 5:12), then atonement by blood will become a necessity to him and his awakened conscience will be satisfied with nothing less.

Atonement by blood is as necessary to God as it is to us. Apart from it His true and full nature and character could never have been known by any of His creatures, least of all by sinful men; but by it His ways are revealed and justified, for it is by the way He has dealt with this question of man's sinfulness that what He is has been fully declared.

## THE DEATH OF THE LORD JESUS: ATONEMENT BY BLOOD

We must face the question as to what God is as well as what we are. Would we have Him to be other than the gospel says He is? In the gospel His righteousness is declared and His wrath is revealed against all ungodliness and unrighteousness of men. Could any creature have security and peace if it were not so? There are those who cavil at God's right to execute justice; would they care to live in a land where crime was strong and law weak? No, they are ready enough to support the law of the land in which they live, and to justify its penalties for their own protection, but deny the right to God to govern and to judge in His universe. Of them the Bible says, "Thou art inexcusable, O man, whosoever thou art that judgest: for thou that judgest doest the same things. But we are sure that the judgment of God is according to truth against them that commit such things" (Romans 2:1-2). How daring and how unreasonable is that spirit in a man which insists upon his neighbour obeying the laws of the land and yet refuses to be subject to the law of God!

Others plead that they are weak and cannot resist temptation to sin, and because of this God must be merciful. But if

> "*weakness may excuse*
> *What murderer, what traitor, what parricide*
> *Incestuous, sacrilegious, but may plead it?*
> *That plea*
> *With God or man will gain thee no remission.*"
> (*"Samson Agonistes"*, John Milton, 1671)

If the judgment of God were not according to truth and justice, if He winked at sin, and were the indulgent, spineless and weak-fatherly being that the modernist would have Him be, then an awakened conscience of a man would be morally greater and better than He, and the devil would take advantage of His weakness and seize

His throne. But we may be thankful and rejoice that God is God, and that His Justice will "never descend from her sceptred royalty" and compound with sin. God will maintain His supremacy and abide for ever and without change in His infinite and unsullied holiness, and all His ways will be in absolute and unchallengeable righteousness.

Since that is so, what of men who are sinful and who have been guilty of rebellion against Him, and as a consequence are lying under the sentence and power of death? There could be no hope for them apart from atonement by blood. Hence the Bible, which is God's Word to men, is full of it; it is, as someone else has said [11], the diamond pivot upon which the New Testament turns, and it is the burden of the Old. It is woven into the very fabric of the Holy Scriptures and is the basis of all relationship between God and sinful men; apart from it there is no light, no peace, no hope for men. If we reject this the Bible has neither message nor meaning for us.

The Old Testament declares, "It is the blood that maketh an atonement for the soul" (Leviticus 17:11), and the New Testament adds its witness by saying, "Without shedding of blood is no remission" (Hebrews 9:22). The coats of skin with which God clothed Adam and Eve in Eden first proclaimed the fact that a victim not chargeable with the offence must suffer in the place of the guilty if he is to go free. Abel's lamb, the ram that was caught in the thicket and offered instead of Isaac, the paschal lamb in Egypt, and all those offerings that were consumed upon Israelitish altars, taught to all who had ears to hear and hearts to understand that there was no other way by which a man's sins could be covered and his transgressions forgiven.

## THE DEATH OF THE LORD JESUS: ATONEMENT BY BLOOD

Yet in those countless altars and sacrifices God had no pleasure. He had no pleasure in Israel's offerings because of the character of those that brought them. "To what purpose is the multitude of your sacrifices to Me? saith the LORD: I am full of the burnt offerings of rams, and I delight not in the blood of bullocks" (Isaiah 1:11). There was no sincerity in the hearts of those who brought them; but the great, the fundamental reason for God's displeasure with them was that the blood of bulls and goats could never take away sin. Hebrews 10 is the great chapter which shows us the futility of these offerings. There we learn that they called sin to remembrance every year, for it is not possible that the blood of bulls and goats should take away sin, and nobody could suppose that they could please God. Then why were they offered? They were a *shadow* of good things to come, and they filled up the period of waiting until the *Substance* appeared. The substance is Christ; it was to Him that all these ancient sacrifices pointed and of His coming they spoke with tongues that were eloquent to the ear of faith. Theories are wearisome, and doctrines are of no value unless they centre in Christ. It is He whom God hath set forth, a propitiation through faith in His blood (Romans 3:25). He is the propitiation for our sins, but not for ours alone, but also for the whole world (1 John 2:2).

The word atonement does not occur in our New Testament, except in Romans 5:11, and it is well known that in that passage it is a wrong translation, and should be "reconciliation". It is an Old Testament word which means "to cover" and does not mean "at-one-ment" as theology declares. It means that the offence is blotted out by the offering; an equivalent is rendered to the aggrieved party which covers the crime. Yet at-one-ment, or to use the fuller, New Testament word, reconciliation, is very closely allied to it, for reconciliation is the result of the atoning sacrifice and death of Christ. By it men are reconciled to God. "For when we were enemies, we were reconciled to God by the death of His Son" (Romans 5:10). This reconciliation is realised when there has been awakened in our souls a sense of need and our eyes are turned upon Him to whom God Himself looks, His Son who died for us, and in Him we have a common object with God.

What an hour that was when the Son of God rose up and coming into the world said, "Sacrifice and offering Thou wouldest not, but a body hast Thou prepared Me: In burnt offerings and sacrifices for sin Thou hast had no pleasure. Then said I, Lo, I come (in the volume of the book it is written of Me) to do Thy will, O God" (Hebrews 10:5-7). We are sure that all heaven was stirred, and the attention of every creature in those realms above was entirely concentrated upon that great event, but who shall tell what it meant to God? His holy will, His glory, the vindication of His character, the revelation of His love were all committed to His beloved Son, to Jesus—the Babe in Bethlehem. And to Him we must look, for the words of the Baptist are as much for us as they were for the crowds that heard them on the banks of Jordan, "Behold the Lamb of God which taketh away the sin of the world."

It has been argued that the doctrine of the atonement is an immoral doctrine, for, according to it, the innocent is compelled to suffer in the place of the guilty. But that is a perversion of the doctrine. When the Son of God came forth to suffer for guilty men, there was no compulsion but that of love. The love of God was the spring and motive of His coming. The well-known John 3:16 would be enough most surely to decide that, but we draw upon

## THE DEATH OF THE LORD JESUS: ATONEMENT BY BLOOD

other texts not so often used, "We have seen and do testify that the Father sent the Son to be the Saviour of the World." "Herein is love, not that we loved God, but that He loved us, and sent His Son to be the propitiation for our sins" (1 John 4:14, 10). "God commendeth His love toward us, in that while we were yet sinners, Christ died for us" (Romans 5:8). And when the Father sent the Son He did not send One who was unwilling to go at His command. "Lo, I come to do Thy will, O God", proves beyond question that His coming was voluntary. He was one with the Father in this, and He took up that body which was prepared for Him by God—He became Man that He might accomplish in manhood all the will of God in regard to men.

Nor did the innocent suffer for the guilty when Jesus died. We cannot attach that word to Him, for it means *without knowledge* of good and evil, and He had full knowledge of all things. He was holy and not innocent; He knew what the sin of man was in its exceeding sinfulness and hated it, and was Himself sinless though a Man; and He knew what the righteousness of God was and loved it, and was God's righteous Servant to manifest and establish it.

Yet He did suffer for the guilty; the Bible tells us this in the plainest language, "Christ also hath once suffered for sins, the Just for the unjust, that He might bring us to God" (1 Peter 3:18). Yes, that is it, "the Just for the unjust", and in that suffering He bore the judgment that the unjust deserved. Atonement is made by the blood which flowed forth from the spear-riven side of Jesus. In virtue of it the sinner is brought to God and by it God is glorified. The love of God and His mercy and grace are exercised in the sinner's salvation in absolute accord with His holiness, righteousness, justice and truth; the majesty of His throne is upheld and His heart flows out in blessing to men; He is a just God and yet a Saviour.

There is the *Godward* aspect of atonement and the *usward who believe* aspect of it. The Godward aspect of it is *propitiation*, which is brought out in Romans 3:25. It was typified in the sin-offering that was consumed without the camp of Israel on the great day of Atonement. The fact that it was consumed outside the camp indicated in figure God's abhorrence of sin, and the great anti-type of that comes out in those solemn words, "He hath made Him to be sin for us, who knew no sin; that we might be made the righteousness of God in Him" (2 Corinthians 5:21). Here, we must confess, is a holy mystery, as deep and impenetrable as was the darkness that for three hours enveloped the cross. But having taken the sinner's place Jesus endured the judgment that was against the sinner, even to being forsaken of God. There was no mitigation of the judgment for Him, but because of who He was, the holy Son of God, He was able to endure and exhaust the judgment, and cry, "It is finished."

The blood of the sin-offering that was burnt without the camp was carried by the high priest into the holiest in the Tabernacle and sprinkled there upon the golden mercy seat and seven times before it, and that was the propitiation, and that was the place where God could meet with His people. Romans 3:24-25 gives the antitype of this shadow. It says, "Being justified freely by His grace through the redemption that is in Christ Jesus: *whom God hath set forth to be a propitiation through faith in His blood.*" The word "propitiation" as used in Romans really means "a mercy seat" or meeting place. And God has set forth Christ Jesus to be this "through faith in His blood". There God in His holiness can meet the sinner in his

## THE DEATH OF THE LORD JESUS: ATONEMENT BY BLOOD

guilt. God is there in free *grace*, but not apart from righteousness, and the sinner may draw near in *faith*.

The *usward who believe* aspect of the atonement is redemption and reconciliation. In Christ, who has so blessedly glorified God about the sin question, "we have redemption through His blood, even the forgiveness of sins" (Colossians 1:14), and we "have been reconciled to God by the death of His Son". Could it be otherwise? All enmity must die out of our hearts as we see God's great desire for our blessing as it has been displayed in the death of His Son, and the more we consider His death the more we are filled with wonder at its suitability to the situation. Nothing else could have met God's claims, nothing else could have met our need; Christ crucified is the power and the wisdom of God and the present and eternal boast of all who are saved.

It should not be difficult to understand that the carrying out of this great work depended wholly upon what the Lord is. If He had not become Man He could not have been our substitute and representative; but having become Man, He was lifted up for us, as Moses lifted up the serpent in the wilderness; and if He had not been the sinless Man He could not have stood for us, for how could one who had sins of his own to suffer for, be a substitute for others? But if He had not been more than man, if He had not been God in His own eternal Being, His sacrifice would have had no atoning value. Who could measure and meet the claims of God's eternal justice but God? Who could understand how sin had challenged the very majesty of God and threatened the stability of God's throne but God? Who could put one hand upon God and one hand upon a guilty sinner, and glorify the One and bless the other, and bring the two together in righteousness and peace, but One who in His own Person was God and man? If He had not been man He could not have died, if He had not been God His death would have been without value.

We rejoice in a full atonement; great peace fills our hearts as we consider it, for what He our Saviour God has done will abide for ever, His blood can never lose its value. We know that by His "one offering He has perfected for ever them that are sanctified", and we know that all things in heaven and on earth are to be reconciled to God on the sure foundation of that same offering. And when that has been effected the throne of God and the Lamb shall be the great centre from which streams of blessing and life will flow to multitudes of men who own the authority of that throne. Thus we return to our beginning, "And He that sat upon the throne was to look upon like a jasper and a sardine stone."

# The Resurrection of the Lord Jesus
## God's Seal upon His Work

The literal resurrection of Jesus was the cardinal fact upon which the earliest preachers of the gospel based their appeal to the Jewish people. Paul, writing to a Gentile church, expressly makes Christianity answer with its life for the literal truth of the resurrection. "If Christ be not risen, then is our preaching vain, and your faith is vain also" (1 Corinthians 15:14). Some modern writers would possibly have reproached Paul with offering a harsh alternative instead of an argument. But Paul would have replied, first, that our Lord's honour and credit were entirely staked upon the issue, since He foretold His resurrection as the sign that would justify His claims: and, secondly, that the fact of the resurrection was attested by evidence which must outweigh everything except an *a priori* conviction of the impossibility of miracle, since it was attested by the word of more than five hundred persons who had actually seen the risen Jesus.—H. P. LIDDON [12].

# Chapter 9
# The Resurrection of the Lord Jesus

## GOD'S SEAL UPON HIS WORK

Never had brighter hopes been buried in any grave than in the grave of Jesus, and never had hearts been more bereft than the hearts of the disciples and of those women that loved and followed Him. How they must have shuddered in their sorrow as the great stone was rolled to its place at the door of the sepulchre, and shut from their tear-dimmed vision the body of their Lord. The night that followed that last Passover feast was a woeful night for them, and for all who loved the Hope of Israel; it was a night unrelieved by any solace from without or faith from within, for having, as they supposed, lost their Lord, they had lost their all and could do nothing but mourn and weep. Yet there was one thing that kept the broken hearts of those women from refusing to perform their office: they would go on the first day of the week and anoint His body. His Kingship had been rejected by the Jews: His claim to it was the charge upon which Pilate had condemned Him to the cross; the multitude had gone to their homes saying, He was no king at all or He would have come down from the cross and saved Himself; but to those women He was King, and more; and though He had lost the kingdom, yet He should lie in His tomb as like a King as they could make it possible. By some means or other they would force their way into that sealed and guarded grave and fill it with the fragrance of the spices that they had prepared, and with the sweeter fragrance of their love; this should be their last tribute to Him, and then they would return—yes, but how, and where, and to what?

Mark tells us that they reached the sepulchre at *the rising of the sun*. Were they blind to the golden glow of that wondrous morning? It is more than likely, for a grave was their goal, and to pour their best upon the dead their purpose; this was the only balm they knew for their death-stricken and hopeless hearts; and what charm could a sunrise have for such as they?

But what a sunrise that must have been, though their eyes did not appreciate it! Let no man tell me that the day dawned as other days, or that all nature did not exult in that great hour. There must have been a triumph and a fragrance in it that never rising of the sun had known before. If when He died—He, the Creator become flesh—the sun drew a veil across its face, and all nature wrapped itself in sable garments, and the earth trembled to its very heart in horror at the deed that men had wrought, there must have been a corresponding joy when the conquering heel of life was placed upon the neck of death, and the shame of the cross was answered by an empty tomb. *"HE IS RISEN."* The glad news had sung its triumphant music to the ends of creation, and "the sun, moon and stars", "the mountains and hills, the fruit trees and cedars", the heavens and the earth were the glorious orchestra that accompanied the angel's proclamation.

## THE RESURRECTION OF THE LORD JESUS: GOD'S SEAL UPON HIS WORK

What wonders greeted those women when they reached the sacred spot. The stone was gone, and instead of Roman soldiers, brutal men who would have found a wretched joy in casting insults at them, they found a heavenly guard in possession, a messenger from God in white apparel. Heaven was not in mourning; its messenger wore the garments of victory and joy, and only waited for human ears to listen to his story. And these women were the first to hear it, and as they heard, the silent chords in their hearts awoke to song, and they turned their backs upon the empty grave, and forgot their useless spices and themselves also, and with fear and great joy did run to tell the tidings. Blessed women, they were the first of ransomed sinners to be swept by the rapture of the resurrection triumph, the first of that countless host whose singing shall be sweeter and more joyous and more prolonged than any raised by sun, moon and stars, or even angels.

The proofs of the resurrection of the Lord Jesus Christ are so many and infallible that nothing but blind unbelief would deny it; but the modernists deny it, they think, like their fathers, the first century Sadducees, that it is an incredible thing that God should raise the dead. The fact is it does not fit in with their evolution doctrines, which doctrines reveal their wish to be free from all responsibility to God. "The wish is father to the thought." The solemn fact of death, not as the debt of nature, but as the wages of sin, the judgment of God upon man because of sin (Genesis 3:17), and resurrection from the dead, which is God's intervention in a scene of death, put an impassable gulf between man and the beasts, and show clearly, in spite of all the efforts of these men to prove the opposite, that their pedigree cannot be traced to a common ancestry. These great facts prove that man was created entirely apart from the beasts, a being accountable to God, and that he has fallen from the high estate in which God set him, and that God only can deliver him from the death that has passed upon him by and through resurrection. But these men rather than bow to the truth of God as to their hopeless sinful state, and receive from Him the life, through Christ, which He as the God of resurrection gives, reject the truth and love the lie. As to resurrection, say some of them, the idea sprang up in the mind of Zoroaster, the Persian philosopher, and that the Jews brought it back from their exile in Babylon, and that the Lord and His disciples incorporated it into their teaching, and that He never rose from the dead.

But the resurrection of the Lord was "according to the Scriptures", Scriptures that existed centuries before Zoroaster breathed. Take the words of David in Psalm 16, "Thou wilt not leave my soul in hell (sheol): neither wilt Thou suffer Thine Holy One to see corruption." We might well ask, Of whom spake David this, of himself or some other man? Not of himself surely, for he was not God's Holy One. Simon Peter, filled with the Holy Spirit on the day of Pentecost, answers our question. "Men and brethren," said he to the assembled Jews, "let me speak freely to you of the patriarch David, that he is both dead and buried, and his sepulchre is with us unto this day. Therefore being a prophet, and knowing that God has sworn with an oath to him, that of the fruit of his loins, according to the flesh, He would raise up Christ to sit on his throne; he seeing this before spake of the resurrection of Christ, that His soul was not left in hell (hades), neither His flesh did see corruption. *This Jesus hath God raised up whereof we all are witnesses"* (Acts 2:29-32).

The resurrection of Christ from the dead which we have most surely believed was predicted by the prophets in the

## THE RESURRECTION OF THE LORD JESUS: GOD'S SEAL UPON HIS WORK

Scriptures and proclaimed by the Apostles who were chosen of the Lord to be the witnesses of it. How interesting and convincing are these witnesses cited by Paul in 1 Corinthians 15. The women are not called, for their evidence in those days would not have greatly counted, but says Paul, "I delivered unto you first of all that which I also received, how that Christ died for our sins *according to the Scriptures*; and was buried, and that He rose again the third day *according to the Scriptures*: and that He *was seen of Cephas*." It was like the Lord to appear first to Cephas; by that act He not only proved that He had risen up from the dead but He showed that He was unchanged in His unwearied grace towards the most failing of His beloved disciples. He was the same Jesus. And this fact had impressed itself upon all the disciples, for we remember how they said when gathered together on the evening of the Resurrection day, "The Lord is risen indeed and hath appeared unto Simon." "The Lord is risen", that was the revelation of His glory, "And hath appeared unto Simon", that was the revelation of His grace. His grace is as great as His glory.

*"Then of the twelve."* Could they be deceived, who knew Him so well? They evidently did not expect to see Him, for when He appeared in their midst they were troubled and affrighted and thought that they had seen a spirit, but His well-known voice dispelled their fear, and when He showed them His hands and feet and side they were glad, for they knew and recognised their Lord. And would they ever forget the peace that filled their hearts in that upper room, when He had said, "Peace unto you"?

*"After that He was seen of above five hundred brethren at once."* This appearance is probably that recorded as having taken place in the appointed mountain of Galilee, where they bowed in worship before Him, though some

doubted. But worshippers and doubters alike had become witnesses, and the greater part of them remained witnesses to the day when Paul wrote of them, at least twenty-five years after.

*"After that He was seen of James"*, who was one of the Lord's brethren, who did not believe in Him in pre-Calvary days, but that sinful unbelief was atoned for by the Lord's death, and dispelled by His appearance in resurrection, so that James delighted to speak of himself as the servant of God and of the Lord Jesus Christ.

*"Then of all the Apostles."* This may not have been that occasion when phlegmatic, unbelieving Thomas fell down at His feet and exclaimed, "My Lord and my God!" but it was an outstanding appearance to which all the apostles bore witness and of which all the Christians talked.

*"Then last of all He was seen of me also"*, not on earth but in the glory of God, exalted to the Father's right hand, but the same Jesus of Nazareth whom men despised and slew, and whom Saul of Tarsus persecuted. What a change that sight of Him made in the persecutor! For him from henceforward the world's prizes were but dross, and his risen living Lord became the sole object of life and love and service for him.

> *"Christ was his end, for Christ was his beginning.*
> *Christ his beginning, for his end was Christ."*

Need we go beyond the witness that Paul added to that of those who were in Christ before Him? except to confirm and seal it all by the Lord's own words to John in the Isle of Patmos. "When I saw Him," said John, "I fell at His feet as dead, and He laid His right hand upon me, saying unto me, 'Fear not: I am the first and the last: I am He that liveth, and was dead; and behold, I am alive for evermore, Amen: and have the keys of hell and death'" (Revelation 1:17-18).

Now consider the alternative that Paul by the inspiration of the Holy Spirit sets before us. He says, "If Christ be not risen, then is our preaching vain, and your faith is vain also. Yea, and we are found false witnesses of God; because we have testified of God that He raised up Christ: whom He raised not up, if so be that the dead rise not … And if Christ be not raised, your faith is vain; ye are yet in your sins" (1 Corinthians 15:14-17).

*"If Christ be not raised"*, the Bible has deceived us, the Gospel is a myth and salvation a dream.

*"If Christ be not raised"*, all faith is vain, there is no forgiveness, we are yet in our sins.

*"If Christ be not raised"*, we who live have no hope, and those who have died have perished.

*"If Christ be not raised"*, sin has prevailed; death has triumphed, and we mourn a defeated Christ.

*"If Christ be not raised"*, the waves of death will flow on without challenge, until the whole race of sinful men has been swept into endless woe.

*"If Christ be not raised"*, God has lost His Son, and men have no Saviour.

*"If Christ be not raised"*, the devil has triumphed, the throne of God is shattered, all light, joy and blessing are blotted out, there will be no peace on earth and no song in heaven.

*"If Christ be not raised"*, those who have prayed, "Thy kingdom come", have prayed in vain; that kingdom will not come, for the kingdom of darkness has won in the great fight, and prayer is a delusion, and faith is folly and

there is no true God, and no living Christ, and we who have believed are of all miserable men the most miserable.

*"But now is Christ risen"*, "who was delivered for our offences and raised again for our justification."

*"But now is Christ risen"*, who had power to lay down His life and had power to take it again, for this commandment He had received of His Father.

*"But now is Christ risen"*, and now the forgiveness of sins is preached to all men, and in Him all that believe are justified from all things.

*"But now is Christ risen"*, and has proved that He was worthy of the trust that God reposed in Him, and has finished the great work which God gave Him to do, and has become the Author of eternal salvation to all who believe.

*"But now is Christ risen"*, and death is defeated; the devil's power is annulled.

*"But now is Christ risen."* He has made a way through death for His ransomed people, and they no longer fear it; they can cry, "O death, where is thy sting? O grave, where is thy victory?"

*"But now is Christ risen*, and become the First-fruits of them that slept." "Every man in his own order: Christ the First-fruits, afterward they that are Christ's at His coming."

*"But now is Christ risen"*, and "Behold, I show you a mystery; we shall not all sleep, but we shall all be changed, in a moment, in the twinkling of an eye, at the last trump: for the trumpet shall sound, and the dead shall be raised incorruptible, and we shall be changed. For this corruptible must put on incorruption, and this mortal must put

on immortality. So when this corruptible shall have put on incorruption, and this mortal shall have put on immortality, then shall be brought to pass the saying that is written, DEATH IS SWALLOWED UP IN VICTORY" (1 Corinthians 15:51-54).

The resurrection of the Lord Jesus is the great witness to His greatness and glory, and to the Father's approval of His life and work on earth. He came forth from the Father to declare to men the great love wherewith He loved them; but they gave Him hatred for love; they despised and rejected Him; they could not endure His presence in the world, and though He was the Lord of glory the princes of this world crucified Him. He was numbered with the transgressors; the cross of a malefactor was the sentence passed upon Him and duly executed by the world. What was God's answer to that? Again and again the Apostles declared God's answer to man's crime. "Ye denied the Holy One and the Just," said Peter to the Jews, "and you desired a murderer to be granted to you; and killed the Prince of Life, *whom God hath raised from the dead*; whereof we are witnesses" (Acts 3:14-15).

We do not wonder that "God hath made this same Jesus both Lord and Christ" (2:36), having exalted Him to His own right hand. The marvel of redeeming love is that thus exalted He should be a Prince and a Saviour to give repentance to Israel, and forgiveness of sins (5:31), not to Israel only, but to every sinner that bows at His feet.

We rejoice and are glad that the Prince of life could not be holden by the power of death. We look within that empty tomb and behold with the wondering disciples the perfect order of it and learn thereby how complete is Satan's defeat, and how signal is God's victory over all the power of death; and we bow in adoration before Him as we believe "the gospel of God concerning His Son Jesus Christ ... declared to be the Son of God with power, according to the spirit of holiness, by the resurrection from the dead" (Romans 1:1-4).

# The Exaltation of the Lord Jesus
## The Answer to His Humiliation

"He that descended is the same also that ascended up far above all heavens, that He might fill all things." This tells us the boundlessness of His sovereignty. In His works, His journeyings, His triumphs, the highest and the lowest regions are visited by Him. He has been on earth and into the lower parts of the earth. He has been in the grave, the territory and the power of death. He is now in the highest heavens, having passed by all principalities and powers. He was received up gloriously, or in glory, as well as into glory. He entered the light of the highest heavens, but He entered it glorious Himself. The real manhood is there; but it is glorified. In Him dwelleth all the fulness of the Godhead bodily. The body that was pierced is that which all eyes shall see. He shall be the eternal object of divine glory and praise and worship.—J. G. BELLETT [13].

## Chapter 10
## The Exaltation of the Lord Jesus

### THE ANSWER TO HIS HUMILIATION

The Old Testament Scriptures hold a riddle that the Jew cannot solve. They looked for—and still look for—a glorious Messiah, the Son of David, but there are many arresting passages in these Scriptures that tell of One who should come in great humility and suffering; who should not be glorious in the eyes of men, but who should in fact be despised and rejected by them. Who could He be? They revelled in such exhilarating prophecies as, "My Servant shall deal prudently, He shall be exalted and extolled, and be very high" (Isaiah 52:13); even the disciples of the Lord looked earnestly for the outshining of that glory, but what could be the meaning of "His visage was marred more than any man, and His form more than the sons of men" (52:14)? It was easy enough to discern the voice of Israel's Deliverer and God in the words, "I clothe the heavens with blackness and I make sackcloth their covering. At My rebuke I dry up the sea" (50:3, 2), but Who is it that says, "I gave My back to the smiters, and My cheek to them that plucked off the hair:

I hid not My face from shame and spitting" (50:6)? Of course, we find the key to the riddle in the New Testament; we know and believe that it is Christ and Him crucified; but this to the Jew is a stumbling-block; he will not have a suffering Messiah and abides in ignorance and unbelief.

It is clear from all Scripture that since man became a sinful, self-centred creature, and death lay upon him as God's judgment, the way to the glory is through suffering; it is "he that humbleth himself that is exalted." I should hesitate to apply the saying, "No cross, no crown" to the Lord Jesus personally, for all the crowns were His according to His rights as the Creator-Son and Heir of all things; yet having descended from the place of His eternal glory and become man for God's glory and our redemption, even He could not reach the joy that was set before Him apart from enduring the cross. He took the downward way of suffering to do the will of God and became obedient unto death, even the death of the cross; it was the only way to the crown.

The disciples of the Lord were as blind to the fact that the way of suffering was the only way to the glory as the rest of the Jews, for when He told them that He "must go unto Jerusalem, and suffer many things of the elders, and chief priests and scribes and be killed, and raised again the third day", Peter took Him and rebuked Him, saying, "Be it far from Thee, Lord, this shall not be unto Thee" (Matthew 16:21-22). He had no conception of God's ways though he understood afterwards when he wrote of the sufferings of Christ and the glory that should follow.

The exaltation of Christ cannot be separated from His humiliation. It is God's answer to all that He suffered in a world dominated by the devil, and as a sacrifice for sins.

## THE EXALTATION OF THE LORD JESUS: THE ANSWER TO HIS HUMILIATION

His own words to His disciples unfolded the story that we love to tell, and which, indeed, had been the burden of all Scripture, "Ought not Christ to have suffered these things," He said, *"and to enter into His glory"* (Luke 24:26), and Peter took up the same theme and enlarged upon it in his Pentecostal witness, "Therefore let all the house of Israel know assuredly, that God hath made that same Jesus, whom ye crucified, both Lord and Christ" (Acts 2:36). And Paul gives the full measure of that exaltation, as the consequence of the descent from Godhead glory to the shame of the cross. "Wherefore God also hath highly exalted Him, and given Him a name which is above every name; that at the name of Jesus every knee should bow: of things in heaven, and things in earth, and things under the earth; and that every tongue should confess that Jesus Christ is Lord to the glory of God the Father" (Philippians 2:9-11).

That Christ is in heaven, a real living man, raised up from the dead, is fundamental to our faith and must be maintained and proclaimed. The Scriptures are so definite about it, that it may seem needless to stress it, but the fact is that multitudes have no knowledge of it at all, they think of Him as a spirit, and not as a man having flesh and bones (Luke 24:39). A young man, a true but unstable Christian, said to me after we had listened to an address on the exaltation of the Lord, "I never knew that Christ was a real, living man in heaven before, I always thought that He was a spirit." I need not say that the knowledge he gained that day changed his life. I think it would be right to say that even as the disciples of the Lord during His life with them thought only of the glory, and in spite of His own words, had no thought of the sufferings, for they were "slow of heart to believe *all* that the prophets had spoken"; so now many sincere Christians think only of the sufferings and do not realise the glory to which Christ has been exalted; they sing, "Simply to Thy cross I cling", and have a very feeble conception of Christ "crowned with glory and honour" at the right hand of the Majesty on high. But our faith is not complete without this, it is the crown of it, and a full, robust and joyful Christian life is impossible if it is not known.

From whichever way we view the ways and counsels of God, whether for His own glory, the blessing of men, or the overthrow of all evil, we see that the exaltation of Christ is a necessity. Take these ways of God on their most simple and elementary ground; that of our blessing. The answer to the challenge, "Who can lay anything to the charge of God's elect?" is "It is God that justifieth." But everything that He does must be according to eternal justice, and how can He justify the ungodly? The answer is *"It is Christ that died"*; by His death a full expiation was made for all our offences. But how do we know that? *"Yea, rather, that is risen again."* His resurrection is God's seal upon the value of His death; the proof that the price paid in it was sufficient. Had it not been, death would have held Him as its prey for ever and even the power of God could not have raised Him. But there is more than resurrection. *"Who is even at the right hand of God."* His exaltation is the declaration of God's entire satisfaction and delight in His work which He accomplished for us. The believer's Substitute and Representative is at the right hand of God. Could He have been there if one sin had remained on Him? Impossible! Yet on the cross He was delivered for our offences; there He was made sin for us; there the Lord laid upon Him the iniquities of us all. Nothing else like His exaltation to the Father's right hand could prove how completely He has borne away "sin's heavy load" for us. The devil himself could not prevent

## THE EXALTATION OF THE LORD JESUS: THE ANSWER TO HIS HUMILIATION

that exaltation and can say nothing against it, and consequently he cannot bring any charge against us for whom Christ suffered and died. But further, *"Who also maketh intercession for us."* If He died and rose again for our justification, He lives and intercedes for us that we might live as justified people (Romans 8:33-34).

It is in Christ that we have redemption; in Him we are justified from all things; in Him we are sanctified, and in Him we have an everlasting, inalienable acceptance with God; but it is in Him who is exalted and crowned in glory, beyond the reach of question or challenge. "This man, after He had offered one sacrifice for sins, for ever sat down on the right hand of God; from henceforth expecting till His enemies be made His footstool" (Hebrews 10:12-13). The value of His death abides; His victory over death by resurrection abides; but He is in the glory and the glory is the answer to the suffering, it is the measure of God's approval of His work, and the pledge of our blessing.

The vindication of the Lord and the subjugation of all evil are involved in this exaltation. Let us consider the words of David in Psalm 110. "The Lord saith unto my Lord, Sit Thou on My right hand, until I make Thine enemies Thy footstool." The Lord used this great saying in His conflict with the Pharisees as a challenge and a warning, giving them thereby an opportunity of discerning who He was and of repenting their enmity towards Him. The words declare His Deity, for they tell us that He was David's Lord, but they also proclaim His exaltation consequent upon His humiliation and rejection by men. Peter takes them up in this way in his Pentecostal appeal to the nation, and his appeal was most powerful; he set two ways open to his hearers, the one was that of surrender to Him whom God had set at His right hand, but refusing that, the other was to be crushed beneath His victorious feet. And it must be one or other for every soul of man.

One most precious feature of our Lord's obedience to His Father's will was His complete committal of Himself to the Father. No thought of self-vindication entered His mind. "He is near that justifieth me" (Isaiah 50:8) was always the spirit in which He moved onward to the cross. When one of His disciples drew a sword to defend Him in the garden, He said to him, "Put up again thy sword into his place ... Thinkest thou that I cannot now pray to My Father, and He shall presently give me more than twelve legions of angels? But how then shall the Scriptures be fulfilled, that thus it must be?" (Matthew 26:52-54). And when at last His enemies had done their worst and He hung rejected and put to shame upon the cross, and the chief priest with the scribes and elders mocked Him saying, "He trusted in God; let Him deliver Him now, if He will have Him; for He said, I am the Son of God" (27:43), He sought no deliverance, and died apparently unheard by heaven. But He was heard. "Thou hast heard Me from the horns of the unicorns" (Psalm 22.21), and His exaltation to God's right hand is God's answer to that complete obedience and perfect trust.

In His life of humiliation He proved Himself worthy to command all things for God; and the Father has given all things into His hands. He has set Him "far above all principality, and power, and might, and dominion, and every name that is named, not only in this world, but also in that which is to come; and hath put all things under His feet, and has given Him to be head over all things to the Church" (Ephesians 1:21-22). And woe be to those who refuse to own His supremacy, be they men or devils. God's will and purposes shall be carried out to the last

## THE EXALTATION OF THE LORD JESUS: THE ANSWER TO HIS HUMILIATION

letter of them and all are centred in Christ in the glory of God.

It is clear that God created the earth as we know it for man's habitation, for His delights were with the sons of men. He crowned Adam as the head of it, giving him a glorious dominion which he was to hold in fief for God. How soon he handed over his dominion to the devil and lost his crown and became subject to death, and every member of his race is like the head of it. Struggle as they may to regain the lost crown, and no matter how great their ambitions and powers, they cannot do it; all their efforts are brought to naught by death, and the crown lies beyond death. Was then God's purpose that man should have this dominion to be frustrated? That could not be; but we must look away from the first man to the Second, from the first Adam to the Last Adam, even as God has done. And we see Jesus, who was made a little lower than the angels for the suffering of death, crowned with glory and honour.

He has gained the crown, but He could only do it through death. By the grace of God He tasted death for everything. He came down into a ruined creation, groaning beneath the curse and the power of death, to remove the mortgage that was on it; He became Man to stand in the place of man who had ruined himself, and to take up all his liabilities and to taste death in all its bitterness that He might destroy its power; and having humbled Himself to the lowest point He has been raised to the highest and all things have been put in subjection under His feet. But not yet is this manifested. This is the "not yet" period, the period of faith. But faith has eyes that see things that are to come, and is assured that they must be, and has the present pledge of them in Jesus crowned with glory and honour.

# Our Great High Priest
## His Qualification for the Office

## CONCERNING HIMSELF

Christ at God's right hand unwearied
   By our tale of shame and sin,
Day by day, and hour by hour
   Welcoming every wanderer in.
On His heart amidst the glory,
   Bearing all our grief and care;
Every burden, ere we feel it,
   Weighed and measured by His prayer.
                —T.P. [14].

# Chapter 11
# Our Great High Priest

## HIS QUALIFICATION FOR THE OFFICE

The closing words of Luke's Gospel are most notable. They tell of the Lord Jesus being carried up into heaven and how His disciples "worshipped Him, and returned to Jerusalem with great joy: and were continually in the temple, praising and blessing God." It is this "great joy" pouring itself out in *worship and praise* that arrests the attention. What was the cause of it? These men were distressed and troubled when they knew that their Lord was going away, and He had to comfort them by telling them of His Father's house and of His coming again to take them there. But when He had actually gone they showed no sign of being bereft, they were not sorrowing orphans, but men brimful and overflowing with confidence and joy. This must be accounted for. It is interesting and instructive to see that this Gospel by Luke opens with a dumb priest in the temple, and closes with these happy worshipping men in the same place. Clearly they were the true priests, offering up spiritual sacrifices to God, even though they were not sons of Aaron. Nothing but a great, and to them unexpected, event could have achieved this miracle.

It is not hard to discover why the official priest was dumb; an angel had brought good news from God to him, and he did not believe it. His dumb mouth was the outward sign of a dumb heart. A sad beginning to the Gospel, but what a joyous close! We catch the spirit of it, and share its gladness as we enquire the reason of it.

The understanding of these men, beloved of the Lord, had been opened to understand the Scriptures. They saw with hearts that believed that the road that Christ had taken was the only road, "it behoved Him to suffer and to rise from the dead the third day." He had fulfilled the infallible Word and glorified God in doing it, and God had given His righteous answer to His suffering and death by exalting Him to His own right hand. They had seen Him go into heaven and they exulted in His triumph, but the way that He had gone must have added to their joy. "He led them out as far as to Bethany"—that showed their willing subjection to His control, He was their Lord and Leader "He lifted up His hands and blessed them"—those uplifted hands and that benediction declared Him to be their great High Priest who had entered into the heavenly sanctuary for them. We must see the meaning of the place into which He has gone and the manner of His going if we are to understand His present High Priestly service. Highest exaltation was His, His going up showed that, but in that exalted place He would not forget them, the manner of His going showed that. No wonder they were filled with joy!

We were not there when He was parted from them and "carried up into heaven", yet the fact is recorded that we might believe it, and vision has been given us by the

## OUR GREAT HIGH PRIEST:
## HIS QUALIFICATION FOR THE OFFICE

Spirit's indwelling, and "we see Jesus, who was made a little lower than the angels for the suffering of death, crowned with glory and honour" (Hebrews 2:9), and we are exhorted to consider Him, the Apostle and High Priest of our profession (3:1). This we will now do.

But first we must see what our profession, or confession, is. We are addressed as "holy brethren, partakers of the heavenly calling." This is our confession. We know that if He had not tasted death by the grace of God for us, and purged our sins by His own blood, and come triumphantly out of death, such a designation and confession could never have been ours. We owe it all to Him. He is our Sanctifier, "for He that sanctifieth and they who are sanctified are all of one" (2:11), He has set us apart for God, even as He has set Himself apart (John 17:19), and we are one with Him; "for which cause He is not ashamed to call us brethren". If we are His brethren we are sons of God and the glory of God is our destiny. This is the revelation of God's grace to us, and being received by faith it sets us in motion towards the glory, and Christ is our Leader in that homeward march; He is the Captain of our salvation. But we need to be sustained and succoured in this way of faith, for we are beset with infirmities and the road is not always easy to travel; we need a great High Priest, to sympathise with us and to succour us and to save us to the uttermost as we come to God by Him; and this great office has been bestowed upon Jesus, our Saviour.

> *"Lord, in all Thy power and glory*
> *Still Thy thoughts and eyes are here;*
> *Watching o'er Thy ransomed people*
> *To Thy gracious heart so dear."*
> (James George Deck, 1802-1884)

It is in the Epistle to the Hebrews that the Lord is shown to us in this attractive way, and it opens with the declaration of His Divine glory: He is the SON. None less than He could have made purgation for our sins, or could lead us to the glory of God. But He had to come down to us and take part in flesh and blood for this, and Chapter 2 plainly teaches the truth as to His coming into manhood. There was nothing lacking in Him as to His eternal Deity. He was the SON. There was nothing lacking in His complete manhood. He was JESUS, and what He was He ever will be. This truth as to His Person is necessary for us; He only, who is God and man in one blessed Person, could be our Saviour, and He only could be our great High Priest. We have trusted Him as our Saviour; we have committed the eternal welfare of our souls to Him, we may with the same confidence rely upon Him to carry us right through to the glory of God by His intercession for us as our great High Priest.

We are dealing now, not with His finished work of atonement, which cost Him those unspeakable sufferings on the cross, but with His present service towards us in heaven: that of being our great High Priest. His finished work on the cross was for sinners, His present work in heaven is for those sinners who have become saints through faith in Him: it is for all who have believed. We read, "Wherefore in all things it behoved Him to be made like unto His brethren, that He might be a merciful and faithful High Priest in things pertaining unto God ... *for in that He Himself suffered being tempted, He is able to succour them that are tempted*" (Hebrews 2:17-18). "For we have not an High Priest which cannot be touched with the feelings of our infirmities; but was in all points tempted like as we are, yet without sin (sin apart, N.Tr.)" (4:15). And again, "Though He were a Son, yet learned He obedience, by the things that He suffered; and being made perfect, He became the Author of eternal salvation unto all them that obey Him" (5:8-9). "But this Man, because He continueth ever, hath an unchangeable priesthood. Wherefore He is able to save them to the uttermost that come unto God by Him, seeing He ever liveth to make intercession for them" (7:24-25).

Here is a theme for our meditation, it is a theme that might well fill volumes printed in gold, but it were better to have it deeply written in our hearts. In pursuing it we are permitted to speak of our great Lord as JESUS, for this precious personal Name occurs many times in this epistle. It is Jesus, who is "the author and finisher of faith" (12:2), which means that He has trodden every step in the way of faith. There is not a trial, temptation, or difficulty in that way that He has not encountered and overcome. That way lay through a world in which all that are godly shall have tribulation, but He overcame the world (John 16:33). He "endured such contradiction of sinners against Himself" (Hebrews 12:3). "He hath suffered being tempted" (2:18), and this because He was *obedient*. Everyone who will be obedient to God shall suffer in a hostile world of which Satan is the god and prince, but His obedience was absolute. Nothing, neither allurements nor terrors, diverted Him from finishing the road upon which He had set His feet for God's glory, and that He might succour us. That road started at the manger—for He said, "Thou didst make Me to hope when I was upon My mother's breasts, I was cast upon Thee from the womb: Thou art My God from My mother's belly" (Psalm 22:9-10), and it ended at the cross, when He cried, "Father, into Thy hands I commend My Spirit" (Luke 22:46).

Of course, there is nothing strange in a servant being obedient, it is his life and duty to obey the word of his master, but the wonder here is "though He were SON, yet learned

He obedience by the things that He suffered." The Son in the Godhead, whose prerogative it was to command and uphold all things by the word of His power, took the servant's place, but He did not cease to be the Son when He did that. He "was made a little lower than the angels for the suffering of death" (Hebrews 2:9), but He was always the Lord of the angels, and they must always worship Him (1:6). Though He took the subordinate place for the will of God, there could not be any question of inferiority as to His Person. How emphatic is the word that the Son is God: "Unto the Son He saith, Thy throne, O God, is for ever and ever" (1:8). And in Chapter 3 we learn that Christ is "Son over His own house", which He has builded, and that "He that built all things is God." I stress this that the wonder of His path of obedience and suffering may grow upon our souls and that we might have a deeper appreciation of the outcome of it.

"Being made perfect, He became the author of eternal salvation unto all them that obey Him" (5:9). He has fully qualified for this, there is not a test that He has not endured and triumphed in. Hence He is able to *sympathise* with those who are enduring trials and testings—for that is the meaning of temptations—and to succour them. He is able to *save* them to the uttermost ... seeing *He ever liveth to make intercession for them* (7:25).

Here is the revelation to us of His unchanging, unwearying love. It has been said, that if it were necessary He would come again from heaven to die for us, so great is His love. That is not necessary, "for by one offering He has perfected for ever them that are sanctified" (10:14), but it is necessary that He should live for us, and intercede for us and succour us; and we should be overwhelmed by the difficulties of the way if He did not. He does this as being moved by the same love that made Him die. The birth pangs do not exhaust the mother's love for her babe; she would be willing to lay down her life for it any time.

> *"Yet she may forgetful prove;*
> *He will never cease to love."*
> (William Cowper, 1731-1800)

To all who obey Him it can be said, "Seeing then that we have a great High Priest, that is passed into the heavens, Jesus the Son of God, let us hold fast our profession. For we have not an High Priest which cannot be touched with the feeling of our infirmities" (4:14-15). He is Jesus, that carries us in thought down to the depths of humiliation and death into which His love carried Him. He is the Son of God, that presents His glory, His magnificent greatness, the splendour of His Person and inheritance. He is Jesus, that tells us of the tender sympathy of His heart for us. He is the Son of God, that tells us of the power of His arm. The tenderest love and the greatest power in the universe abide in Him. He is Jesus, that tells of His preciousness to us. He is the Son of God, that tells us of His preciousness to God. Since He is Jesus, He loves us so well that there is nothing that would be good for us that He will not ask for when He intercedes before God for us; since He is the Son of God, there is nothing that He asks for us that God will deny.

Having such a great High Priest we are exhorted to draw near to God with boldness. First for the help we need in all the ups and downs of life, and second, to be worshippers before Him. We must not confound these two drawings near; they are distinct, and separated one from the other by five chapters in our Epistle. First, having such a sympathetic High Priest, we are exhorted "Let us come boldly to the throne of grace, that we may obtain mercy, and find grace for timely help" (4:16). We are put into contact by our High Priest with the inexhaustible resources of divine grace, and we have but to ask at the throne of grace, and that succour that we need in the hour of trial will be supplied. We could not have a better illustration of this than Paul, when the thorn in the flesh oppressed him so sorely. Should it be taken away? that was his desire; or would he give way under it? that was Satan's desire, but it was unthinkable. The Lord soothed his spirit with infinite sympathy and succoured him with all-sufficient grace.

We see how Simon Peter missed this wonderful sustainment because of his self-confidence. He did not cry to the Lord in the hour of trial as Paul did, and he fell. Yet even he was preserved from despair by the intercession of the Lord. "Simon, Simon," said the Lord, "Satan hath desired to have you, that he may sift you as wheat: but I have prayed for thee, that thy faith fail not" (Luke 22:31-32). Paul and Peter were the objects of the tender solicitude of the Lord, as all His saints are. He interceded for them before the trial seized them. Paul was preserved from failure, and Peter was preserved in spite of failure. Grace to keep and grace to restore came to them through the Lord's priestly activities on their behalf. We might take another illustration from Peter's experience. He walked on the water to go to Jesus, and found that the circumstances were such as he could not overcome, and he began to sink. But when he cried out in fear and need the Lord stretched forth His hand and held him up, and he walked on the waves by His support. No picture could set forth more beautifully the gracious succour that is ministered now to those who are conscious that they have no help outside the Lord. He stretches forth the hand of a man to their aid, but in that hand is the power of God.

But He is not only our great High Priest to succour us in our weaknesses, He is over the house of God, and He would have us draw near with boldness, not to the throne of grace only, but into the holiest, into the very presence of God, where not our needs are in question but where God's glories shine forth. We have the title to enter there, and we may do so with hearts full of thanksgiving, without any fear, being fully assured that it is God's delight that we should be there, having our conscience clear of all sense of guilt through the one efficacious offering that Christ has made, and our whole beings consecrated to Him whose love has won our hearts (Hebrews 10:19-22). This is the great present end of the service of the Lord as our great High Priest, and we ought not to be indifferent as to it. It is sad that we would so often avail ourselves of the means without reaching the end, glad to have the relief that the grace gives, but not pressing on to have God as our exceeding joy and the object of our hearts' adoration.

Those men of Luke 24 were in the joy of this in spirit, they do not seem in that glad hour to have had anything to pray for, it was all overflowing praise and worship with them. They had to pray later, and they did pray with real purpose, and we shall need to pray every day, but there is this other side, so near to the heart of God. He would have us draw near for His own sake and not simply because we have needs. He would have us near Himself because He loves us greatly and He desires that our love should flow out to Him in response.

Time and space fail us to pursue this great subject now but "of the things we have spoken this is the sum. We have such an High Priest, who is set on the right hand of the throne of the Majesty in the heavens" (Hebrews 8:1), and this glorious person is Jesus the Son of God who loved us and gave Himself for us (Galatians 2:20), and who ever liveth to make intercession for us (Hebrews

7:25). May we be stirred up to know the Lord and His present gracious activities on our behalf in a fuller measure.

# The Deity of the Lord Jesus
## IN THE LATER EPISTLES

The Son is true God, seated on a throne of divine perpetuity, and maintaining a moral government of matchless and inflexible rectitude, Himself immutable and eternal. He must remain in peerless majesty when the material universe shall have passed away; through all intermediate periods ensuring the triumphs of His church, until every enemy shall be crushed beneath His feet.— R. Treffry, Jun. [15].

# Chapter 12
# The Deity of the Lord Jesus

## IN THE LATER EPISTLES

It is not in Paul's later Epistles only that the truth of the Deity of our Lord is emphasised, it is the fountain from which all his ministry flowed. "It is taken for granted all through his Epistles, and is the very soul and marrow of the entire series of doctrines. When this is lost sight of, all is misshapen and dislocated but when this is recognised, all falls into its place as the exhibition of infinite power and mercy clothed in a vesture of humiliation and sacrifice, and devoted to the succour and enlightenment of man" (Liddon [16]). The divine glory of his Lord was everything to Paul. We surely realise this as we read of his heroic life of labour and zeal and endurance and sacrifice, and consider his burning words. From the hour when his astonished eyes saw Him in the glory and heard His voice as he lay stricken by His power on the road to Damascus, the enthroned Jesus was the object of his faith and love and life, and he yielded to Him an allegiance that only God could claim. He delighted to speak of himself as His bond slave; to count the greatest prizes that the world could give as the dust beneath his feet and well lost for the excellence of the knowledge of Christ Jesus his Lord. He preached Him as the subject of the gospel of God, and called upon men to repent Godward, and to believe in the Lord Jesus Christ for their soul's salvation as they would believe in God. He charged the princes of this world with crucifying *the Lord of glory*, and boldly declared, "If any man love not our Lord Jesus Christ let him be anathema" (1 Corinthians 16:22). He spoke of Him as our "great God and Saviour Jesus Christ" (Titus 2:13) and as the "Judge of the quick and dead" (2 Timothy 4:1). How awe-inspiring are his words in 2 Thessalonians 1: "The Lord Jesus shall be revealed from heaven with His mighty angels, in flaming fire taking vengeance on them that know not God, and that obey not the gospel of our Lord Jesus Christ: who shall be punished with everlasting destruction from the presence of the Lord and from the glory of His power." Of whom could such words have been written but of the eternal God?

But it is not difficult to see how necessary it was that the truth should be stated in definite terms in the later epistles, not only for those to whom they were first addressed but for us also. The deity of Christ is the central fact of our Faith; it is the glory of it and that that gives stability to our souls and enables us to endure to the end; and it is that which is the object of the most persistent attacks of Satan. Fierce was the war that raged about it in the early centuries of the Christian era, and to this day the test of everything is "What think ye of Christ, whose Son is He?" If He is David's Son, "How then doth David in spirit call Him Lord?" (Matthew 22:42-43). How good it is that we are not left to the vagaries of the Fathers, or to the opinions of modern theologians, or to our own deductions and conclusions, but that we have the clear, definite, unequivocal words of Holy Scripture for what we believe.

# THE DEITY OF THE LORD JESUS: IN THE LATER EPISTLES

## THE HEBREW EPISTLE

The faith of the Hebrew Christians was being sorely tried; they had hoped that their nation would have accepted Christ as the Messiah, but only a feeble remnant had done so, and they were between two fires, persecuted by pagan Gentiles and reviled by their own countrymen. And just ahead of them lay the destruction of Jerusalem and their dispersal to the ends of the earth. The time had come for a complete and final break with all that they had held most sacred—priests, sacrifices, temple, city. What could carry them through this time of sore trial and maintain them stedfast in the faith? One thing—the transcendent glory of their Lord and Saviour. Hence their need was the occasion for the Spirit of God to take of the things of Christ and show them to them, and to glorify Him (John 16:14), and to clothe Him with distinctions and glories which belong only to the eternal God. How wonderful are the opening words of the Epistle, "God who at sundry times and in divers manners spake in times past unto the fathers by the prophets, hath in these last days spoken unto us in His Son, whom He hath appointed Heir of all things, by whom also He made the worlds; who being the brightness of His glory and the express image of His person, and upholding all things by the word of His power, when He had by Himself purged our sins, sat down on the right hand of the Majesty on high." Lack of space and time prevent me from attempting to say anything about this range of glories that could belong to no creature however exalted, but surely the contemplation of them must bow every believing heart in wonder and worship at His feet, and especially so as we realise that it is Jesus, who died for us, to whom these glories belong.

But there is one passage in the chapter that we must consider. It is a quotation from Psalm 102. "And Thou,

Lord, in the beginning hast laid the foundation of the earth and the heavens are the works of Thy hands. They shall perish; but Thou remainest; and they all shall wax old as doth a garment, and as a vesture shalt Thou fold them up, and they shall be changed, but THOU ART THE SAME, and Thy years shall not fail" (Hebrews 1:10-12). Who can this be who creates for His own glory, and who, when what He has created has served His purpose, folds it up and sets it aside like a worn-out garment, but who abides Himself in His own eternal, immutable, unchanging Being? Who can He be? Let the end of the Epistle answer the question. "JESUS CHRIST THE SAME yesterday, to-day and for ever" (13:8). Consider this declaration of His glory. The words were addressed to Him when as man on earth His strength was weakened in the way and He drew near unto death. It was one Person in the Godhead addressing another, and addressing Him, as the words indicate, as the Alpha and the Omega, the beginning and the end, the first and the last, the One whose creatorial voice called time into being and who will have the last word about every thing; who when former things have passed away and time has ceased to be, will say, "Behold I make all things new." "It is done" (Revelation 21:5-6).

Consider what the effect of the contemplation of this glorious Lord must have had upon these sorely harassed Hebrew Christians; and shall we be less affected? It is He who has said, "I will never leave thee nor forsake thee" (Hebrews 13:5). As He said of old to Jacob the wanderer (Genesis 28:15), to Joshua the warrior (Joshua 1:5), and to Solomon the worshipper (1 Chronicles 28:20), so He says to us, and what strong consolation His word gives, for it is impossible for Him to lie. So that we may boldly say, as those Hebrews could say, "The Lord is my helper, I will not fear what man shall do unto me" (13:6).

## COLOSSIANS 1

I have been impressed with the fact that those Scriptures in the Epistles that make reference to our Lord's pre-incarnate being, present Him to our faith as the Son and as the Creator. As the Son He stands in relation to the Father and as the Creator He stands in relation to time and all that He has created. And I am sure that it would be right to say that the universe was made and is upheld by His power that He might fill it with the blessedness of that love wherewith the Father loved Him before the foundation of the world.

In Colossians 1:13 it is said that the Father "hath delivered us from the power of darkness and hath translated us into the kingdom of the Son of His love" (N.Tr.). This is the only time that the Kingdom of the Father's Son is so named in Scripture; there must be a reason for it. The reason for it, and for the divine glories of the Son that follow, is to be found in the danger that menaced the Faith at Colosse. A subtle foe was bent upon seducing the faithful brethren in that Church from Christ. He was insinuating that while it was well enough to have Christ they would be none the worse off for a little of the world's philosophy. Christ and Plato would make an admirable mixture; and if they would borrow from Jewish ordinances and curb their Christian liberty by a discreet asceticism they would be gainers in every way. The best of Judaism's ritual, and the best of Greek thought would enrich their faith. But the whole effort was to displace Christ in their souls and blind them to His eternal oneness with the Father, and to reduce Him in their thoughts to the level of a created being. And this also is the trend of modern thought in Christendom. Even the missionary is told that he must no longer go forth proclaiming the Name of Jesus as the only name in which there is salvation, for there is good and truth, say they, in all religions, and the Moslem and the Hindu have also got messages for mankind and they should meet together with the Christian on equal terms and pool their respective wealth. In view of these efforts to degrade the Son of God, how necessary to us is the Epistle to the Colossians.

How necessary it was that Paul should arise in his loyalty to his Lord, and in bold, God-given words declare the peerless, unassailable glory of Christ, for only that could preserve the saints of God from this deadly error in his day, and nothing else can do it in this. The truth of God does not change, Christ does not change: the Son of the Father's love is from everlasting to everlasting, and He is the Head of His body the Church, and must have no rival. In all things He must have pre-eminence.

We read that "by Him were all things created, that are in heaven, and that are on earth, visible and invisible, whether they be thrones, or dominions, or principalities, or powers: all things were created by Him and for Him; and He is before all things, and by Him all things consist" (Colossians 1:16-17). "*By Him.* The force which has summoned the worlds out of nothingness into being and which upholds them in being, is His; He wields it; He is the one Producer and Sustainer of all created existence. *For Him.* He is not as Arianism afterwards pretended, merely an inferior workman, creating for the glory of a higher Master, for a God superior to Himself; He is the End of created things as well as their immediate Source, and in living for Him every creature finds at once the explanation and the law of its being. For 'He is before all things, and by Him all things consist'" (Liddon [16]).

## THE DEITY OF THE LORD JESUS: IN THE LATER EPISTLES

We surely realise the infinite character of His glory and wisdom as the Creator, yet as the Son He has a greater glory, a glory that surpasses all creature comprehension. As the Creator He is supremely above every creature that He has made, and that supremacy will yet be confessed by every creature in heaven, on earth and under the earth; but the Name of Son declares what He was to the Father before any creature existed. "The Son of His love"; "the only-begotten Son which is in the bosom of the Father". "Thou art My beloved Son in whom I am well pleased." "Having one Son, His well-beloved". How these words move the heart, and bow us down before the Father, especially when we read that it is into the kingdom of His Son that we have been translated through grace. Some have endeavoured to explain the mystery of this eternal relationship between the Father and the Son, and have made deductions and arrived at conclusions which have been neither wise nor helpful. I will not do that, it is better to accept what is written without asking, How? For "no man knoweth the Son but the Father."

> *"The higher mysteries of His fame*
> *The creature's grasp transcends.*
> *The Father only that blest Name*
> *Of Son can comprehend."*
> (Josiah Conder, 1789-1855)

What is beyond all controversy is that He, the Son, was loved by the Father before the world's foundations, and that the Father sent Him forth, made of a woman. He gave His only-begotten Son, that the love of the eternal relationship might be revealed to us, who without it would have remained in the power of darkness for ever.

The kingdom of His Son is a kingdom of light, and outside of it is darkness. It is a kingdom of light because "He is the image of the invisible God", "the brightness of His glory, and the express image of His Person". "The only-begotten Son which is in the bosom of the Father, He hath declared Him." He is the One who represents God to the universe He has created, and He will flood His kingdom with the knowledge of God. Adam was created as in God's image in a minor way, but he was but a figure of Christ. It is THE SON who is the true image, and God is fully revealed in Him, not as Father only, though that surely is the most blessed part of this divine revelation, but all that the eternal God is has found its expression in Him, for "all the fulness (of the Godhead) was pleased to dwell in Him"—the despised Nazarene, and now "all the fulness of the Godhead dwells in Him bodily" (Colossians 1:19; 2:9, N.Tr.). All the light of God for His universe streams from His beloved Son. All else is darkness whether it be Judaism, Grecian philosophy, Hinduism, Mahomedanism, or that Modernism that while holding to the Christian name denies the Father and the Son. For "whosoever denieth the Son, the same hath not the Father" (1 John 2:22-23). And John, inspired by the Holy Ghost, uses strong language of such. He says they are liars and antichrists. He is the true Light, the Light of the world, and shineth for every man, but "the god of this world hath blinded the minds of them that believe not, lest the light of the glorious gospel of Christ who is the image of God should shine unto them" (2 Corinthians 4:4).

Great and varied are the glories that He bears in this chapter, glories upon which no creature could lay his hands, or claim a title to. He is the Redeemer; the Image of the invisible God; the Creator of all things, and the End for which they were all made, and He sustains the universe that He has made by His almighty and undiminished power. In Him the fulness of the Godhead was pleased to dwell, and by an infinite sacrifice He has made peace so that He will as a result of it, and by His own divine power, reconcile all things on earth and in heaven to God, and bring them into harmony with the central throne. But these glories belong to Him because of who He is; they are names and renown that none but He could have gained, but before He rose up and went forth to glorify God in any of them He was the Son of the Father's love. He is this in His own eternal Being. And those who have believed have been brought into His kingdom, into subjection to Him, and as being in that kingdom they are indwelt by the Holy Spirit, the Spirit of God's Son; and they are loved with the love wherewith the Father loved Him, for said He, "I have declared unto them Thy Name, and will declare it: that the love wherewith Thou hast loved Me may be in them and I in them" (John 17:26).

"Beware", then, since such a glorious Lord and Saviour and Head is yours, O Christian, "lest any man spoil you through philosophy and vain deceit, after the tradition of men, after the rudiments of the world, and not after Christ. For in Him dwelleth all the fulness of the Godhead bodily. And ye are complete in Him, which is the Head of all principality and power" (Colossians 2:8-10).

*CONCERNING HIMSELF*

# The Son of Man
## THE JUDGE OF QUICK AND DEAD

Heaven is opened, and a white horse appears, the familiar figure of war and victory. It is upon the Rider that our eyes are fixed. He is called "Faithful and True", and in righteousness He judges and wars: His warring is but itself a judgment. For this, His eyes penetrate as a flame of fire; nothing escapes them. Many diadems are on His head—the sign of absolute authority—and worthily, for His Name in its full reality, expressing His nature, is an incommunicable one, beyond the knowledge of finite creatures. His vesture is dipped in blood, for already many enemies have fallen before Him. And His Name is called—has been and is, as the languages implies—"the Word of God". The Gospel of John shows us that in creation already He was that, and now in judgment He is no less so.— F. W. GRANT [17].

# Chapter 13
# The Son of Man

## THE JUDGE OF QUICK AND DEAD

"The only-begotten Son which is in the bosom of the Father" became THE SON OF MAN that He might fulfil the whole will of the Triune God. His title of Son of Man is a glorious title. It carries with it universal dominion, as we should expect, seeing He is who He is, and yet the first occurrence of it in the New Testament is in those memorable words of His: "The foxes have holes, and the birds of the air have nests: but *the Son of Man hath not where to lay His head*" (Matthew 8:20). It was into such poverty that He who will rule all things for God came for God's glory and the salvation of men. Before taking the dominion and power, He trod the way of service and suffering. He gently rebuked the pride and ambitions of His disciples with the words, "Even as *the Son of Man* came not to be ministered unto, but to minister, and to give His life a ransom for many" (20:28). Yet He knew what the result of His sojourn on earth would be, for even in the darkest hour of His life, when arraigned for blasphemy before the high priest of His people, and when "they did spit in His face, and buffeted Him; and smote

Him with the palms of their hands" He said, "Nevertheless I say unto you, Hereafter shall ye see *the Son of Man* sitting on the right hand of power, and coming in the clouds of heaven" (26:64).

As *the Son of Man* He was lifted up, even as Moses lifted up the serpent in the wilderness. It was a necessity, without which His kingdom would have been a barren kingdom, with never a man in it to rejoice in His glory. He was lifted up as the representative of men to bear the judgment that lay upon them that He might be the Redeemer before He takes the throne as Judge. But as surely as He was lifted up upon the cross, so surely will He fill the throne, for "The Father ... hath given Him authority to execute judgment also, because He is *the Son of Man*" (John 5:26-27).

He has been "ordained of God to be the Judge of quick and dead" (Acts 10:42). So Peter declared in the first gospel sermon ever preached to Gentile hearers, and I should connect the judgment of the living with His title Son of Man. He will judge the dead also at the end of Time at the great white throne, for "the Father hath committed all judgment to the Son that all men should honour the Son even as they honour the Father" (John 5:22-23), but He will do that in His Divine majesty. It is before God that the dead, small and great, shall stand (Revelation 20). HE IS GOD.

As Son of Man He will deal with the living when He comes. Then He will wield the SICKLE, the SWORD and the SCEPTRE. He is seen with the sickle in Revelation 14:14-16. "And I looked," says John the Apostle, "and behold a white cloud, and upon the cloud one sat like unto *the Son of Man*, having on His head a golden crown, and in His hand a sharp sickle ... and He that sat upon

## THE SON OF MAN:
## THE JUDGE OF QUICK AND DEAD

the cloud thrust in His sickle on the earth, and the earth was reaped."

He came into the world to sow the good seed of the kingdom, for "He that soweth the good seed is *the Son of Man*" (Matthew 13:37). That sowing cost Him more than mortal tongue shall ever tell. He fulfilled the word "He that goeth forth and weepeth, bearing precious seed". Aye, not only were "strong crying and tears" His portion, but blood also. "The seed is the word of God", the full revelation of what God is, and He had to die to sow that seed; and He who sowed the seed must reap the harvest; and the latter part of that ancient word will also be fulfilled—"Shall doubtless come again rejoicing, bringing His sheaves with Him" (Psalm 126:6).

But tares have been sown in the wheat field; this was the work of an enemy, and that enemy was the devil (Matthew 13:39), and the Son of Man must discriminate between wheat and the tares; so we read that "He shall send forth His angels and they shall gather out of His kingdom all things that offend, and them that do iniquity". As the wielder of the sickle He will execute a discriminating judgment. To use another forceful figure, that of the rugged Baptist, "His fan is in His hand, and He will throughly purge His floor, and gather the wheat into the garner; but He will burn up the chaff with unquenchable fire" (3:12).

That passage probably has Israel specially in view, but this discriminating judgment will be extended to the Gentile nations as Matthew 25:31-32 teaches. "When *the Son of Man* shall come in His glory, and all the holy angels with Him, then shall He sit upon the throne of His glory; and before Him shall be gathered all nations: and He shall separate them one from another, as a shepherd divideth his sheep from the goats." It is strange that so many theologians should have interpreted that passage as being the great final judgment of the dead, until which none could know whether they would stand on the right hand of the Lord or the left, saved or lost, say they. It is clear enough that it is the judgment of *living nations* at the appearing and glory of the Son of Man, and that will take place at the beginning of His reign of a thousand years over the earth, while the final judgment of the *dead* will take place when those thousand years are finished (Revelation 20).

The Son of Man will bring in the glory and the blessing; the angels of God shall ascend and descend upon Him (John 1:51). He will bring down heaven to earth for "He shall come down like rain upon the mown grass" (Psalm 72:6). But note well the figure. It is upon the *mown* grass that He comes down. The sickle will have done its work first. The sharp sickle in the hand of the gold-crowned Son of Man will be thrust into the earth when God's work and the devil's shall be fully ripe.

We are not surprised that as their Master went up to Jerusalem for the last time His disciples followed Him amazed and afraid. Their forebodings must have been greatly increased when He said to them, "Behold we go up to Jerusalem, and *the Son of Man* shall be delivered unto the chief priests and scribes, and they shall condemn Him to death, and shall deliver Him to the Gentiles: and they shall mock Him, and shall scourge Him and shall spit upon Him and shall kill Him" (Mark 10:33-34). Could it be the same Son of Man whom John saw in Patmos, shining in His divine Majesty? Yes, it was the same. There is none other who could go down to such depths and be exalted to such heights; and He is the Ancient of Days. Even John's eyes could not look upon such glory as was there revealed in Him, nor could he stand upon his feet before Him. He says, "When I saw Him, I fell at His feet as dead." Nor would he have known Him as his beloved Lord if He had not laid His right hand upon him with a well-remembered tenderness, and in tones of compassion said, "Fear not; I am the first and the last; I am He that liveth and was dead; and, behold, I am alive for evermore, Amen; and have the keys of hell (hades) and of death" (Revelation 1:12-18).

The keys of death and hades in His hand declared that He, the Son of Man, is the undisputed Master of the unseen world, even though His authority is challenged by living men. But He is coming to judge the living, for "out of His mouth went *a sharp two-edged sword* with which He would smite the nations" (1:16 and 19:15).

THE SWORD must precede the sceptre because of what men are. How strange is that popular delusion that the world is to be gradually converted by the gospel, or that the kingdom of God will be evolved by men's own efforts out of the world as it is. Hear what the Scripture says: "Behold He cometh with clouds; and every eye shall see Him, and they also that pierced Him: *and all kindreds of the earth shall wail because of Him*" (1:7). Even so. Amen. A converted world would welcome Him with acclamation; a godless world will wail with terror at the sight of Him. The sword first and then the sceptre. That sword indicates resistless justice: the vengeance of God upon unrepentant, wicked men. It will compel every stubborn knee to bend and every rebellious lip to confess that Jesus is Lord to the glory of God the Father. "Gird Thy sword upon Thy thigh, O most mighty, with Thy glory and Thy majesty. And in Thy majesty ride prosperously because of truth and righteousness: and Thy right hand shall teach Thee terrible things" (Psalm 45:3-4).

It seems almost an incredible thing that men should assemble together to make war on Him who is King of kings and Lord of lords, yet they will, and such is the delusion with which the devil will delude them that they will hope to achieve their purpose and keep Him for ever out of this world. So we read, "I saw the beast, and the kings of the earth, and their armies gathered together to make war on Him that sat upon the horse, and against His army" (Revelation 19:19). They will stretch forth their hand against God, and strengthen themselves against the Almighty: and in their blind hatred they will run upon Him, "even upon the thick bosses of His buckler" (Job 15:25-26). But the battle will be swift and decisive, for the sword of the Son of Man shall prevail, and the blasphemous leaders of that vast host of men shall be seized by divine power and cast alive into the lake which burneth with fire and brimstone, "And the remainder shall be slain with the sword of Him that sat upon the horse, which sword proceeded out of His mouth, and all the fowls of the air were filled with flesh" (Revelation 19:20-21).

THE SCEPTRE of the Son of Man will be an iron sceptre and for it He has been in great conflict. It has been the devil's purpose from the beginning to oppose His wielding it. He must have understood and taken to heart God's words to him in the Garden concerning the woman's Seed. "It shall bruise thy head and thou shalt bruise His heel" (Genesis 3:15), and he has spared no force or wile that he hoped would prevent this. He was not ignorant of the times, for the time of the Advent of the woman's Seed had been plainly told in Old Testament Scripture and when that time came, he "stood up before the woman (Israel) which was ready to be delivered, for to devour her child as soon as it was born. And she brought forth *a man*

## THE SON OF MAN:
## THE JUDGE OF QUICK AND DEAD

*child* who was to rule all nations with a rod of iron" (Revelation 12:4-5). Failing in that first onslaught, he changed his tactics, and masked his guns and advanced with a flag of truce and terms of peace. We read, "The devil taketh Him up into an exceeding high mountain, and showeth Him all the kingdoms of the world and the glory of them; and saith unto Him, All these things will I give Thee, if Thou wilt fall down and worship me." But the Lord knew him for the adversary that he was, and answered, "Get thee hence, Satan; for it is written, Thou shalt worship the Lord thy God, and Him only shalt thou serve" (Matthew 4:8-10).

He refused the short and easy way to the throne and sceptre that Satan offered Him at such a price, and took instead the way of obedience to the will of God, and God's will was the death of the cross. He showed Himself worthy to rule by complete subjection. "Though He were a Son, yet learned He obedience by the things that He suffered" (Hebrews 5:8). He loved righteousness and hated iniquity, and the sceptre of His kingdom will be for ever a sceptre of righteousness. But He would take that sceptre neither from the devil nor men, but from the hand of God only. We learn this from Daniel's night visions. Said he, "I saw in the night visions, and behold, one like *the Son of Man* came with the clouds of the heaven, and came to the Ancient of Days, and they brought Him near before Him. And there was given Him dominion, and glory, and a kingdom, that all people, nations and languages should serve Him: His dominion is an everlasting dominion, which shall not pass away, and His kingdom that which shall not be destroyed" (Daniel 7:13-14).

A corresponding scene to that is found in Revelation 5: "And I beheld, and lo, in the midst of the throne and the four beasts (living creatures) and in the midst of the elders stood a Lamb as it had been slain, having seven horns and seven eyes, which are the seven Spirits of God sent forth into all the earth. And He came and took the book out of the hand of Him that sat upon the throne" (5:6-7). In John's vision He receives the sickle and the sword from the hand of God, and in Daniel's vision He receives the sceptre. The LORD had said unto Him, "Ask of Me, and I will give Thee the heathen for Thine inheritance, and the uttermost parts of the earth for Thy possession. Thou shall break them with a rod of iron; Thou shalt dash them in pieces like a potter's vessel" (Psalm 2:8-9). He would have nothing and take nothing except from the hand of God; in this He is in striking contrast to the first man, Adam, who grasped at something that God in His wisdom had withheld from him, and fell into disaster and death.

God intends that the proclamation of His coming kingdom of righteousness shall go out in testimony to the Gentiles. It was announced by Paul to the Athenians on Mars Hill, when He said, "God now commandeth all men everywhere to repent: because He hath appointed a day, in the which He will judge the world in righteousness by that Man whom He hath ordained; whereof He hath given assurance unto all men, in that He hath raised Him from the dead" (Acts 17:30-31). He is the King that shall reign in righteousness and the work of righteousness shall be peace; and the effect of righteousness, quietness and assurance for ever (Isaiah 32).

Marvel not that the sickle and sword and sceptre should be put into the hands of the Son of Man. He only of all men who have appeared on earth could wield them in undiminished righteousness and power. Every other man to whom power and authority had been given had failed; Adam, Noah, Moses, David, Solomon, Nebuchadnezzar,

## THE SON OF MAN:
## THE JUDGE OF QUICK AND DEAD

all broke down when tested, and have had to make way for the Son of Man. He has prevailed and will never fail, for in His absolute dependence upon God He has been upheld, and the word has been fulfilled and will yet be fulfilled: "Let Thy hand be upon the Man of Thy right hand, and upon THE SON OF MAN whom Thou madest strong for Thyself" (Psalm 80:17). Again I quote His own words: "Marvel not at this: for the hour is coming, in the which all that are in the graves shall hear His voice, and shall come forth; they that have done good, unto the resurrection of life; and they that have done evil, unto the resurrection of damnation" (John 5:28-29). "Blessed and holy is he that hath part in the first resurrection: on such the second death hath no power." "But the rest of the dead lived not again until the thousand years were finished" (Revelation 20:6, 5).

Then will come the final judgment, which John describes in awe-inspiring words. "And I saw a great white throne, AND HIM THAT SAT ON IT, from whose face the earth and the heaven fled away; and there was found no place for them. And I saw the dead, small and great, stand before God and the books were opened; and another book was opened, which is the book of life; and the dead were judged out of those things which were written in the books, according to their works. And the sea gave up the dead which were in it; and death and hell delivered up the dead which were in them: and they were judged every man according to their works. And death and hell were cast into the lake of fire. This is the second death. And whosoever was not found written in the book of life was cast into the lake of fire" (20:11-15).

He will lay aside the sickle when its work is done; He will lay aside the sword when its work is done, and when as Son of Man He has glorified God in His kingdom He will hand back to God the sceptre, for we read, "Then cometh the end, when He shall deliver up the kingdom to God, even the Father; when He shall have put down all rule and all authority and power. *For He must reign, till He hath put all enemies under His feet.* The last enemy that shall be destroyed is death. ... And when all things shall be subdued unto Him, then shall the Son also Himself be subject unto Him that put all things under Him, that God may be all in all" (1 Corinthians 15:24-28).

## References

[1] John Nelson Darby (1800-1882), *"Luke 1"*, *Synopsis of the Books of the Bible*, T. H. Gregg, London, 1857

[2] Handley Carr Glyn Moule (1841-1920), *"Prefatory Note"* to Sir Robert Anderson (1841-1918), *The Lord from Heaven*, J. Nisbet & Co., London, 1910

[3] John Nelson Darby, *"Matthew 1"*, *Synopsis of the Books of the Bible*, T. H. Gregg, London, 1857

[4] John Nelson Darby, *"Matthew 3"*, *Synopsis of the Books of the Bible*, T. H. Gregg, London, 1857

[5] John Nelson Darby, *"Matthew 4"*, *Synopsis of the Books of the Bible*, T. H. Gregg, London, 1857

[6] Samuel Ridout (1855-1930), *Lectures on the Epistle to the Hebrews*, Loizeaux Bros, New York, 1903

[7] Henry Parry Liddon (1829-1890), *"Lecture V: The Doctrine of Christ's Divinity in the Writings of St. John"*, *The Bampton Lectures for 1866*, Fourth Edition, Rivingtons, London, Oxford and Cambridge, 1869

[8] Sir William Robertson Nicoll (1851-1923), *The Incarnate Saviour: a life of Jesus Christ*, T. & T. Clark, Edinburgh, 1897

[9] Edward Gibbon (1737-1794), *The History of the Decline and Fall of the Roman Empire*, W. Strahan & T. Cadell, London, 1776-1789

[10] James Boyd (1851-1936), *"The Cross"*, *Scripture Truth*, Volume 1, 1909, p.290

[11] James Denney, D.D. (1856-1917), *Studies in Theology: Lectures delivered in Chicago Theological Seminary*, Fourth Edition, Hodder & Stoughton, London, 1895

[12] Henry Parry Liddon, *"Lecture IV: Our Lord's Divinity as Witnessed by His Consciousness"*, *The Bampton Lectures for 1866*, Fourth Edition, Rivingtons, London, Oxford and Cambridge, 1869

[13] John Gifford Bellett, *The Son of God*, W H Broom, London, 1869, quoting from John Owen, *Christologia or a Declaration of The Glorious Mystery of the Person of Christ, God and Man*, 1679

[14] T.P., translated by Frances Bevan (1827-1909), *Hymns of Ter Steegen, Suso and Others,* J. Nisbet & Co., London, 1894

[15] Richard Treffry, Junior (1804-1836), *An Inquiry into the Doctrine of the Eternal Sonship of our Lord Jesus Christ*, John Mason, London, 1837

[16] Henry Parry Liddon, *"Lecture VI, Our Lord's Divinity as taught by St. James, St. Peter, and St. Paul"*, *The Bampton Lectures for 1866*, Fourth Edition, Rivingtons, London, Oxford and Cambridge, 1869

[17] Frederick William Grant (1834-1902), *"Part 7, The Consummation, Book 2—"Things That Shall Be"*, An Exposition of Revelation 4-22", *The Revelation of Christ to His Servants of Things That Are, and Things That Shall Be*, Loizeaux Bros, New York, 1894

# Other Books from Scripture Truth Publications

**UNDERSTANDING THE OLD TESTAMENT SERIES:**

HOW TO OVERCOME BY JOHN T MAWSON
*ISBN 978-0-901860-62-0 (paperback)*
*144 pages; April 2009*

DELIVERING GRACE BY JOHN T MAWSON
*ISBN 978-0-901860-64-4 (paperback)*
*ISBN 978-0-901860-78-1 (hardback)*
*192 pages; March 2007*

**UNDERSTANDING CHRISTIANITY SERIES:**

"WAITING FOR THE COMING" BY JOHN T MAWSON
*ISBN 978-0-901860-67-5 (paperback)*
*130 pages; February 2011*

THOU REMAINEST BY JOHN WILSON SMITH
*ISBN 978-0-901860-04-0 (paperback)*
*100 pages; December 2013*

www.ingramcontent.com/pod-product-compliance
Lightning Source LLC
Chambersburg PA
CBHW060155050426
42446CB00013B/2834